SECRETS OF

Italian Pasta

OVER 100 AUTHENTIC PASTA RECIPES

General Editor · Beverly LeBlanc

Macdonald Orbis

A *Macdonald Orbis* BOOK

Based upon *La Pentola d'Oro*, © Editoriale Del Drago, Milan 1983
English text and design © Macdonald & Co (Publishers) Ltd 1986, 1988
First published in Great Britain in 1988
by Macdonald & Co (Publishers) Ltd
London & Sydney

A member of Pergamon MCC Publishing Corporation plc

British Library Cataloguing in Publication Data
LeBlanc, Beverly
   Secrets of Italian Pasta
    1. Cookery (Macaroni)
   I. Title
   641.8'22   TX809.M17

ISBN 0-356-15317-7

Illustrated by Claire Harper

Designer: Clair Lidzey

Macdonald & Co (Publishers) Ltd
Greater London House
Hampstead Road
London NW1 7QX

Printed and bound in Great Britain by
Purnell Book Production Ltd, Paulton, Bristol
A member of BPCC plc

CONTENTS

Introduction 7

Italian Wine 8

Italian Cheese 12

Pasta 16

Sauces 73

Soups 87

Index 94

Symbols

The symbols show how easy a recipe is, and the preparation and cooking times:-

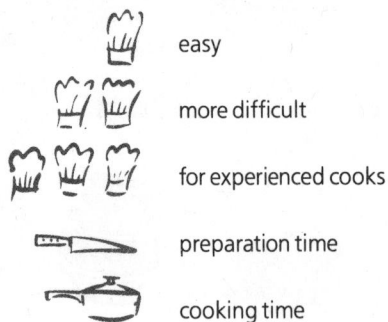

easy

more difficult

for experienced cooks

preparation time

cooking time

When using this book, remember the following points: (1) all quantities are for four people unless otherwise stated (2) use only one set of ingredients for the recipes, since American, imperial and metric ingredients are not exact equivalents and (3) in the text of the recipes, American quantities and ingredients are listed first, with the British equivalents in square brackets.

INTRODUCTION

For more than a thousand years, following the disintegration of the Roman Empire, Italy was divided into armed camps and a fragmented assortment of independent states. The terrain contributed to this isolation between states with natural barriers, like the Alps and the Apennines, discouraging travel. When unification was finally achieved great regional differences in cultural and culinary traditions still remained. These traditions have helped to preserve an Italian cuisine which is rich in variety and ranks amongst the finest in the world.

French cooking owes much to the refinement of Italian cooking and historians claim this dates from the marriage of Catherine de Medici to Henry II of France. It was said that, until then, French cooking was similar to that of the rest of northern Europe. However, Catherine brought with her a contingent of Italian cooks who introduced many innovations to the cooking of the French court. The Italian cuisine of the sixteenth century, in the upper echelons of society, was superbly elegant. This must be in part attributed to the geographic position of Italy and the wide-ranging mercantile interests — these brought the spice trade which had a lasting influence on the local ingredients and the way in which food was prepared.

The common idea that Italian food consists of pasta, pizzas and dishes doused in garlic is far from the truth — indeed much of the food in Northern Italy, apart from Piedmont, uses little or no garlic. Italian vegetables are amongst the best in the world and the discerning housewife in Italy expects to buy tender young vegetables. These feature largely in the antipasti, the first course of Italian meals, which is a seemingly endless variety of hors d'oeuvres and snacks.

In spite of the regional differences which abound throughout Italy there is one common concept, the selection of good-quality, fresh ingredients. This is essential in a cuisine that endeavours to produce food which, while often simple, is always excellent, making it absolutely impossible to disguise inferior produce.

ITALIAN WINE

Few countries in the world possess such a diversity of wines as Italy. The sheer variety of tastes to be found in Italian wines reflects the ebullience of its volatile, warm-natured people. In every region there are producers striving to make the best wines of the area, each convinced that he has found the key to the whole art of winemaking and produced a wine that will eclipse that of his neighbor. The result is a mosaic of flavors and bouquets, wines with personality and character, and an abundance of bottles to choose from for all who appreciate *la cucina italiana*.

Some Italian wines are produced on mountain slopes, others by the side of one of its many lakes. There are those from the searing heat of the south, while others hail from northerly climes of hard winters and wide temperature fluctuations. Over the centuries, the grape varieties suitable for each area have evolved, giving the wines their 'regional' flavor and identifiable character, even when tasted without looking at the label. Still other producers are blazing a trail and planting grape varieties hitherto unknown in their area, creating new, splendid wines which have surprised everybody.

Then there is the controversy of DOC versus non-DOC. In 1963, when Italy wanted to expand its wine exports (still only about a quarter of annual production is exported), a law was created to control the name and origin of many of its wines—DOC. Today, the 200 DOC zones produce nearly double that number of styles of wine, but only about 10 per cent of production is Denominazione di Origine Controllata. The DOC law is roughly similar to the French Appellation Contrôlée, in that it controls the grape varieties which a producer can use, delimits growing zones, lays down rules for winemaking and ageing, and sets out other parameters a wine must meet in order to be awarded DOC. This encourages quality, but cannot guarantee it — the integrity and knowledge of the producer himself, and his desire to make or keep a reputation for himself, are the best guarantee of quality. There is also a 'super' category of DOC, DOCG or Denominazione di Origine Controllata e Garantita, with some more stringent rules attached to its acquisition. But the name of a good producer is still the best insurance of all. DOCG labels are starting to appear on Barolo, Barbaresco, Brunello di Montalcino, Vino Nobile di Montepulciano and Chianti.

However, the words Vino da Tavola, or Table Wine, still appear on a mass of other wines. This can be because the wine is one which carries a brand name, rather than a regional designation, but some Vino da Tavola labels refer to the color of a wine and its place of origin, or the grape variety and the place from which it comes. There are a number of Italian wines which bear the modest title of Vino da Tavola which are amongst the finest bottles in the land. This may be because the producer has decided to experiment and make wines from grapes which are not typical of his area, hence foregoing the designation DOC, or because he has voluntarily opted out of the DOC system in order to follow, for instance, his own ideas on ageing his wine (perhaps using small barrels), or to open up some new land not hitherto used for viticulture and therefore outside the DOC zone.

It used to be said that there was an enormous difference, immediately discernible on the nose and the palate, between the wines of the north and the south of Italy. Although this is still true of the reds, where some of the richest, most heady examples come from the sun-drenched south, it is becoming more difficult to tell the difference between whites from the north and those from the south. This is due to modern vinification, or winemaking methods which have tended to produce the fresh clean wines we now like, rather than the slightly heavy, sometimes oxidised examples of yore. If a white wine is fermented at cold temperature, easy to control in large tanks, the result will be youthful flavor, whether the grapes originally came from Sicily or the northern half of the country.

However, as in any winemaking area of the world, the innate quality of the grape variety used will greatly influence the wine which is ultimately made. There are many grape varieties in Italy which are indigenous to the country and which are not found anywhere else. But there are regions in Italy where a number of grape varieties are shared with France and Germany, especially in the north-eastern part of the country. This includes the Cabernet, that famous variety of grape grown with great success in the Bordeaux region of France, California and Australia, and which is now finding favor in the northern vineyards and further south in Tuscany and Umbria.

The best way to consider the wines of Italy, in a limited space, is in relation to Italian food. For this is the context in which Italians themselves see their wines, since they regard wine as an intrinsic part of any meal and expect to marry their regional dishes to their vinous partners. But we need not be so bound by regional distinctions, for we have the whole map of Italy at our disposal. The Italian rarely moves out of his own region when choosing his wine, but with the vast array of Italian wines now in the world's shops, we can be more adventurous. The trick is to see the potential of a dish when married to a wine, to play with contrasting and matching tastes, to understand the nature of the dish being prepared and to know what wine will enhance it.

I have attempted to select some original ideas and to juggle with them, so that there will be some exciting taste combinations and gastronomic experiences. I will deliberately 'name names', so that good producers get the credit they deserve and you can see wines which are among the best examples of their kind. Nothing is definitive in wine, especially not in Italian wine terms where improvement is constant and new discoveries frequent, but if these suggestions send you rushing to a good wine shop, then they will have achieved their purpose. Italian wine and food are for the sensually curious, for those who like the challenge of tastes and flavors, and if some of these wines open up new avenues of gastronomic pleasure, then the liquid research on your behalf will have been worthwhile.

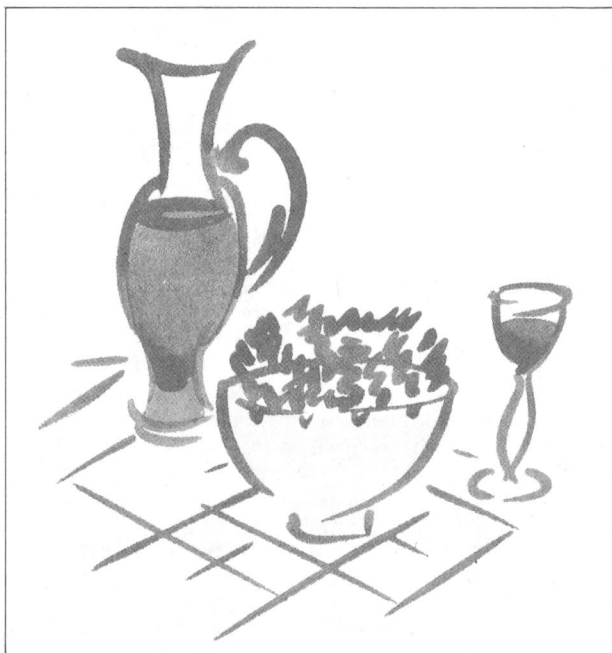

Wine with pasta

Of course, it is the sauce of the pasta, rather than the pasta itself, that decides the wine. Classic spaghetti bolognese, or the Roman spaghetti carbonara, with bacon and egg sauce, call for vivid, young, fruity red wines. A vibrant Merlot or Cabernet di Pramaggiore would be ideal. This is the area on the borders of the Veneto and Friuli-Venezia Giulia, and here the wines have a sappy charm which is attractive — try those from Santa Margherita or Tenuta Sant'Anna.

The hot arrabbiata sauce with peppers, beloved by southerners, poses a few problems. Sicilian red can be the answer, whether it is Regaleali, Corvo, or the Etna red from Villagrande. The Romans like their pasta 'all'amatriciana' with tomatoes, bacon and sweet pepper. What better than a young Latium red wine, Velletri, to go with it? The Castelli Romani, or Roman hills, produce more white wine than red, but Velletri rosso is eminently quaffable.

A gorgonzola sauce has become popular with spaghetti, and here the choice of wine may depend on the type of cheese used, the sweet or piquant gorgonzola. The saltiness of the stronger cheese certainly calls for white wine — red wine is always slightly 'emasculated' by salt. Anything labelled Pinot

Bianco would be a perfect partner, from Lombardy, Trentino-Alto Adige, the Veneto, or Friuli-Venezia Giulia. With the sweeter gorgonzola, or as an accompaniment to any of the pasta dishes with a cream sauce, try a young white Trebbiano di Romagna from that great gastronomic region, Emilia-Romagna. Producers to rely upon include Ferrucci and Fratelli Vallunga, both of whom also make fine white Albana and red Sangiovese di Romagna.

Pesto, that heavenly basil, garlic and cheese sauce, is another test for the wine buyer. The obvious answer is a Ligurian white, and here the most historic is Cinqueterre. But it is not what it used to be, and a young, fresh Vermentino would probably give much more pleasure. The same grape variety gives a Vermentino di Alghero from Sardinia — the firm of Sella & Mosca are unrivalled in their modern techniques and attention to quality.

Baked lasagne is quite a heavy dish, and a light red usually presents a good contrast — young Valpolicella, or maybe a young Dolcetto d'Alba from Piedmont. Most good producers of Barolo and Barbaresco make a Dolcetto, which could be termed the Beaujolais of Italy, with the Dolcetto grape replacing the Gamay and fulfilling the same role as a soft, fruity wine for youthful drinking. A favourite Dolcetto d'Alba comes from Baracco de Baracho.

Where filled pasta is concerned, whether it be ravioli or tortellini, it all depends on what is in the filling. A tortellini filling of Parma smoked ham, turkey and Bologna mortadella, for instance, would go beautifully with the Romagnan variety of the red grape, Sangiovese. Drink it young, but if you have a filling of stronger meats, you could pair it with a Sangiovese di Romagna Riserva Superiore with more bottle age, perhaps from Spalletti (Rocca di Ribano). Veal is often used to fill ravioli — a young Bardolino would be ideal here. With a ricotta or a spinach filling, my preference would be for a fruity white, maybe a Tocai from Grave del Friuli. Tocai has nothing to do with either the Tokay of Hungary or the Tokay/Pinot Gris of Alsace, but it is a soft, fruity white wine, sometimes quite rich.

One of Italy's greatest treats is to serve pasta, and sometimes gnocchi, with slivers of the precious white truffles of Piedmont. A layer of truffle slices, often grey and not very appetizing in appearance, nevertheless gives off an earthy, root-like smell, quite unlike any other. What wine can match this? I have found Pinot Grigio, that intriguing, slightly aromatic grape variety, excellent in matching the humus-like flavor of truffles, and one one of the best is that of Jermann in the Collio area of Friuli-Venezia Giulia. It works, also, when truffle slivers are put over Parma ham or the incomparable Bresaola. Other Pinot Grigio wines of class come from Attems, Schiopetto, Gradnik, Villa Russiz, Formentini and the Felluga family. Occasionally a Pinot Grigio will have a pinkish tinge to it, which means that the skins have been left in contact with the fermenting wine, producing extra body, flavor and bouquet. This is an experience not to be missed.

ITALIAN CHEESE

Cheese has always been an integral part of Italian life. The ancient Romans were said to be nauseated by the idea of drinking milk so they ate it instead in an astonishing variety of cheeses. Fresh, smoked or dried cheeses were available; cheeses curdled with fig juice or flavored with nuts or spices and herbs like mint, coriander or marjoram and made with cow's or ewe's milk, even with goat's milk from Liguria. And there was a cheese called Lunar, of the Grana family which includes those aristocrats of Italian cheese, Grana Padano and Parmigiano Reggiano, better known in its grated form as Parmesan.

Today, cheese plays just as important a role in Italy's way of life; the milk and cheese industry occupies a valuable position in the economy, representing about a quarter of the agricultural gross saleable product. Over half the milk produced in Italy is used to make cheese and although small farmers and firms continue their tradition of cheese-making, large companies and cooperatives have grown to meet the demands of home and export markets. The authorities strive to ensure that ancient traditions and accepted quality are maintained in the face of necessary refinements and innovations in production, packing, presentation and marketing techniques.

Italian cheeses are protected by specially appointed consortiums which define and protect from imitation those cheeses with a clearly defined 'name of origin' or 'Zona Tipica'. They ensure that standards are maintained in both production and marketing and the penalties for fraud include prison sentences and fines of up to 50,000 or 100,000 lire.

A cheese with 'zona tipica' is a product of a unique nature which has a specific quality in terms of use and is of known popularity or fame. It also indicates that a cheese comes from a particular area with specific geographical limits and that the product owes a large part of its quality characteristics to the particular environment of that area, taking into consideration human, historical and cultural factors.

It is geographical factors which influence greatly the diversity of Italian cheese. The alpine pastures to the north, just south of the Swiss and French borders, house such prolific cheese-producing regions as Fruili-Venezia Giulia, Trentino and Veneto, and the centre of the Italian cheese industry, Lombardy with Piedmont to the west and Emilia Romagna to the south-east of the lush Po Valley renowned for cow's milk cheeses. Moving further south, the regions of Tuscany, Lazio, Campania and Puglia and the isles of Sardinia and Sicily produce excellent sheep's milk cheeses, sheep being twice as numerous as cattle in Italy, particularly in the South. Goat's milk cheeses, once numerous, are becoming a rarity now and even Caprini, the small and delicate cheeses once made from goat's milk (capra means goat) are now made almost entirely from cow's milk. Individual farmers and concerns produce occasional goat's milk cheese but they are not mass produced.

Indeed the individuality, profusion and variation of Italian cheeses can make their identification and selection most confusing. Practically every corner of Italy can boast a cheese speciality and on a wider scale the same cheese can be sold under different names.

Alternatively, the same name can apply to many cheeses which are totally different in character. So it is the true connoisseur who can confidently find his way round the cheese boards of Italy. Happily, when it comes to exports, the situation is not quite so confusing although the availability of certain cheeses can vary enormously from city to city. All the major cheeses mentioned in this section are available either in supermarkets or specialist shops although some may be difficult to find in remote areas. Many of the lesser-known cheeses may be difficult to buy and are mentioned purely for interest and information.

The best known Italian cheeses, apart from *Grana Padano* and *Parmesan* which have already been mentioned, are: *Gorgonzola*, Italy's principal blue-veined cheese; *Dolcelate*, a milder blue cheese; *Mozzarella*, traditionally made from buffalo milk; *Fior di Latte*, the official name for Mozzarella made with cow's milk; *Taleggio*, a popular mild and aromatic semi-soft cheese; *Pecorino Romano*, a strong-flavored sheep's milk cheese imported mostly by the U.S.A.; *Ricotta* which is not really a cheese but is produced by re-treating the ewe's milk whey after making cheese, often Pecorino, and of which there are many types and flavors; *Mascarponi*, versatile and delicious almost pure whipped cream cheese; *Robiola*, a soft, creamy cheese sometimes likened to Camembert; *Burrini*, specialist cheeses hand molded around a pat of butter; and *Cacetti*, similar to Burrini, without the butter filling.

There are numerous variations to these cheeses produced by individual companies or farms. Gorgonzola, for instance, is produced sometimes with creamy Mascarponi or perhaps with anchovies or caraway seeds or walnuts; Mascarponi itself can be mixed with a variety of other cheeses, maybe Robiola, sometimes with truffles, or herbs, or mixed seasonings; one company produces Mascarponi with cognac while in Tuscany, Ricotta Ubriaca or 'drunken ricotta' is what you get when the cheese is mixed with brandy or rum!

Types of Cheese

Bel Paese

This unpressed, cooked and ripened cheese was created by Egidio Galbani in 1906 and made at Melzo in Lombardy. It is one of the most popular cheeses of this century and is creamy white or pale yellow, soft, buttery and elastic, without holes but with a pleasant, tangy flavor. The name, meaning beautiful country, was taken from a book written by Abbot Antonio Stoppani, a friend of the Galbani family, whose portrait, imposed on a map of Italy, appears on the foil wrapping of some of the exported cheeses; others depict a map of the western hemisphere.

Mozzarella

Mozzarella is a soft, pliable, porcelain white cheese made since the sixteenth century in southern Italy from the milk of the water buffalo. Now it is often made from a combination of cow's and water buffalo's milk and where it is made entirely from cow's milk, such as in the north, it is called Fior di Latte.

There are various types of Mozzarella. For instance from the hills of Rome in the Abruzzi region, comes a type of cow's milk Mozzarella called Scamorza, sometimes smoked. In the traditional areas of the South, the buffalo milk cheese is sometimes smoked also using wheat straw, leaves or wood, and is called Smoked Mozzarella di Bufala or Smoked Provola di Bufala.

Gorgonzola

This is another exceptional product from the Po Valley and is said to be even older than Grana cheese.

It is named after the town where it is believed to have originated but is no longer made, not far from Milan. It is produced now at both local and mass production level in the provinces of Bergamo, Brescia, Como, Cremona, Cuneo, Milan, Novara, Pavia, Vercelli and the area of Casale Monferrato. A protected cheese, it is produced all the year round and is Italy's major blue-veined variety. It has a characteristically strong flavor from its compact, creamy texture and is white or straw colored with green flecks. The rind is a natural, rough, reddish-grey color.

Mascarpone

Mascarpone is a delicious creamy dessert cheese, almost like pure cream whipped into a light, velvety consistency. It is served either with food or on its own, flavored with cinnamon, powdered chocolate or liqueurs.

Mascarpone was originally made only in Lombardy in the autumn and winter but now it is available all the year round and is usually sold in muslin bags or in tubs.

Parmigiano Reggiano or Parmesan

This undisputed king of Italian cheese is believed to have originated in the province of Reggio Emilia south of the Po Valley. The area was formerly under the rule of the Dukedom of Parma which was the main trading centre, hence its name. It was called the great cheese of seven countries because the ancient formula remained unchanged throughout 700 years of history which altered the face of continents.

Fontina

A very popular Italian cheese, genuine Fontina comes from the Valle d'Aosta in the north-west and plays an important part in the cuisine of that area. It is made from the full cream milk of once-milked cows with acidity produced by natural fermentation.

The cheese is medium-hard although its flesh is soft and melts easily. It is straw colored with a mild and delicate flavor while its rind is soft and pliable either light brown or slightly orange. It is ripened for about three months and each cheese is marked with a circle containing an outline of the Matterhorn (which majestically marks the borders of Italy and Switzerland) with 'Fontina' written in the centre. The cheese has been likened to Swiss Gruyère but it is sweeter and softer.

Pecorino Romano

Pecorino is the generic term for cheeses made with ewe's milk (pecora means sheep) and this is one of the most important of Italian cheeses associated particularly with central and southern Italy. It is a hard-cooked (boiled), drum-shaped cheese made from fresh, full cream sheep's milk curdled with lamb's rennet and it has a decidedly strong flavor. There are numerous local variations but the most prominent of these, dating back to the first century BC, is Pecorino Romano.

It is because of these qualities which allow the cheese to keep so well that its export market has grown consistently. Although it is only made between November and June, production is on a very large scale and the cheese is, of course, protected by law.

Ricotta

Ricotta is not really a cheese but is obtained by re-treating whey, although nowadays whole or skimmed milk is sometimes added to produce a richer product. Ricotta cheeses are made from sheep's or cow's milk although the ewe's milk cheeses are considered the best, particularly Ricotta Romana di Pecora, and the cheeses from the regions of Tuscany, Sardinia and Sicily. They are often made from left-over Pecorino whey.

Basically, it is an ivory white cheese with a delicately sour flavor and an after-taste of milk. The fresh cheese is very soft, bland, unripened and unsalted, whereas older cheeses, salted and dried, may be matured for sixty days or more to produce a dry, hard cheese for grating. There are also smoked cheeses and some produced only on special occasions.

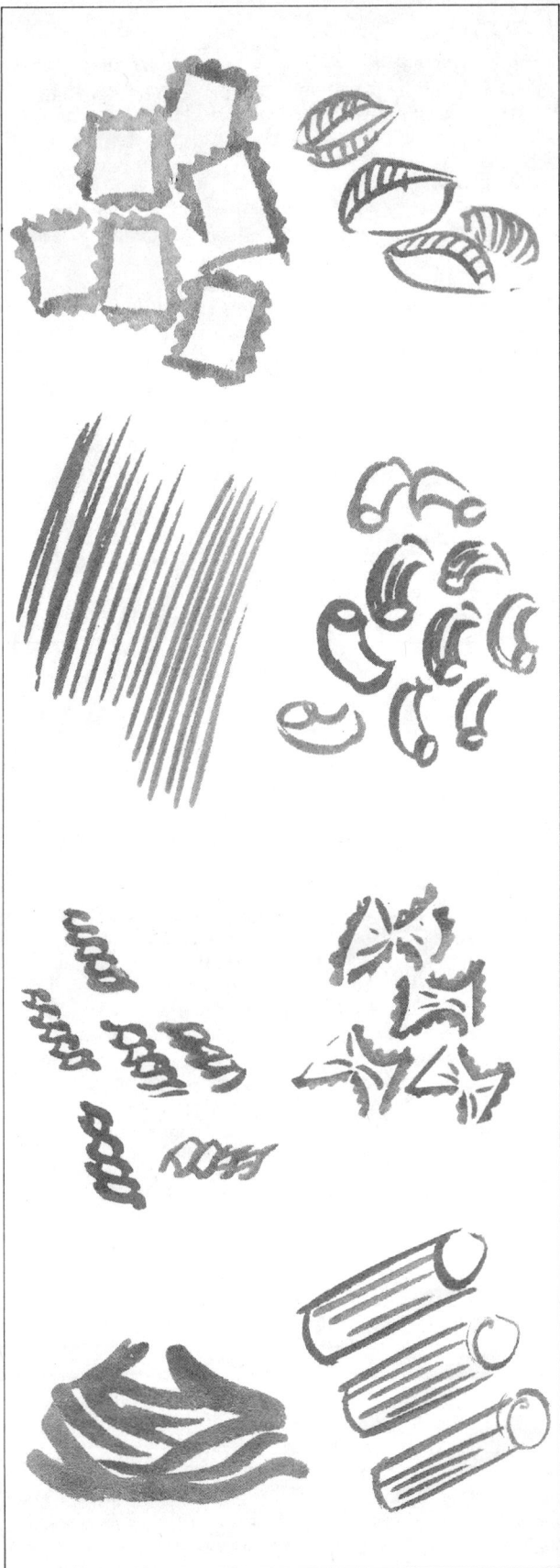

PASTA

Pasta is one of the most versatile of foods; it comes in an incredible range of shapes and sizes and can be filled or unfilled, can be eaten in soup or boiled or baked. The best pastas are made with hard durum wheat – *semola di grano dúro*. Dry pasta, *pasta secca*, is made with flour and water; *pasta all'uovo* has the addition of eggs, green pasta is flavored with spinach. Pasta comes in cords, tubes, flat noodles (some of which come in nests), some pastas are smooth, others are wavy or ridged. The best known of the cord pastas are spaghetti and vermicelli, and macaroni of the tubular ones. Noodles range from the tiny tagliarini to the wide lasagne and there are tiny fancy shapes to eat in soup – stars, bow ties, letters of the alphabet, butterflies, thimbles and umbrellas. Some of the most versatile pastas for salad are elbow macaroni and shells. If you are going to use pasta in a cold salad, rinse it in cold water after it has been cooked and drained. This stops the cooking and chills the pasta ready for tossing with the dressing.

If you have the patience, you can make fresh pasta and there are electric machines which make pasta very quickly. Fresh pasta cooks in half the time of dried pasta.

In Italy, there are firm traditions about which sauces go with which pasta shape – shellfish are usually served with thin spaghetti, hollow shell shapes and tubes with meat sauces. However, the only limitation is that of the cook's imagination. Our recipes are simple and the choice of pasta is flexible. It is up to you, how you mix the different pastas and flavors. Purists will tell you that the only cheeses to serve with pasta are parmesan and pecorino romano. But gruyère, comté or emmental cheese go well with it, as do mozzarella, bel paese, port-salut, fontina, fontal or raclette.

To cook pasta
Allow 3-4oz [75-125g] of pasta per person. Fill a very large, deep saucepan with water, allowing about 1 quart [1½ pints] of water and when it comes to a boil, add a good spoonful of salt and 1 tablespoon oil then the pasta little by little as the water comes back to a boil. Cooking time for spaghetti is about 10-12 minutes. When cooked, it should be *al dente*, that is, still quite firm when bitten into, so taste it before removing from the saucepan. As soon as the pasta is cooked, drain it and place immediately in a dish with the sauce.

Cook's tip: these are the basic cooking times for different kinds of durum wheat pasta: vermicelli – 3 minutes; spaghetti, 10-12 minutes; shells, 10-12 minutes; macaroni, 15-20 minutes; cannelloni, 15-20 minutes. If you are cooking fresh pasta, it will take about half the time of dried pasta.

Opposite: *a selection of pasta showing just some of the many shapes that are available. From left to right starting at the top:-*
Ravioli, *filled pasta which looks like large postage stamps*
Conchiglioni, *seashell-shaped pasta*
Spaghetti, *solid rods of pasta which are classified according to their size and include capellini, fidelini, spaghettini, and spaghettoni*
Small Macaroni; *small but ridged macaroni is called riglioni*
Marziani, *or malloredus, looks like coiled springs*
Farfalle, *butterfly-shaped pasta, is also called cravattine or bow ties*
Tagliatelle *comes in nests of various widths*
Cannelloni, *a large tube of pasta, is usually filled with a meat or vegetable sauce.*

Pasta con semolino

Pasta with Semolina

	01:00		00:05
	plus 00:30 in refrigerator		

American	Ingredients	Metric/Imperial
1 lb	Semolina, finely ground or all purpose (strong white) flour	450 g / 1 lb
5	Eggs	5
1 tbsp	Salt	1 tbsp
	Flour	

1. Put semolina in a heap on the pastry board, make a hole in the centre and put in eggs beaten with salt. Begin to knead with your hands, forming a ball-shaped mixture. Work until dough is smooth and even. Continue kneading dough firmly until bubbles form on the surface. Wrap ball of dough in foil and put in the bottom of the refrigerator for 30 minutes.
2. Remove and knead again for about 10 minutes. Flour pastry board and roll out dough, not too thinly. Leave dough to dry, turn over and dry on the other side, then cut into shape.
3. Cook in plenty of boiling salted water with a few drops of oil until 'al dente', cooking time according to shape.

Cook's tip: unless you can get very finely ground semolina it is better to use plain white flour. Allow 3-4 oz / 75-125 g of pasta per person.

Pasta al formaggio

Pasta with Cheese

	01:30		00:03 to 00:08

American	Ingredients	Metric/Imperial
2 cups	Reggiano or parmesan cheese	225 g / 8 oz
2 cups	Flour	225 g / 8 oz
5	Eggs	5
1 tsp	Salt	1 tsp

1. Finely grate cheese and mix with the flour, then tip onto a pastry board. Make a well in the centre. In a bowl beat one of the eggs with salt and pour into the well.
2. Flour hands, begin to knead mixture, add another beaten egg, knead again and continue this process until all eggs are added, to produce a smooth even dough.
3. Break dough into several pieces kneading each piece well, then reshape all pieces together to form a smooth ball. Wrap in transparent film or seal in a plastic bag and leave in a cool place (not the refrigerator) for 1 hour.
4. Flour pastry board, put dough in centre, flatten with a rolling pin and turning over the dough frequently, roll into a thickish rectangle. Cut into required shape and cook immediately in plenty of boiling salted water. Cooking time will depend on shape and thickness of the pasta.

Pizzoccheri

Pizzoccheri

A typical dish from the mountain pastures of Valtellina.

01:00   00:20

American	Ingredients	Metric/Imperial
3 cups	Buckwheat flour	350 g / 12 oz
1 ½ cups	White flour	175 g / 6 oz
4	Eggs	4
½ cup	Milk	125 ml / 4 fl oz
	Salt	
½ lb	Potatoes	225 g / 8 oz
½ lb	French beans	225 g / 8 oz
½ cup	Butter	100 g / 4 oz
1 tsp	Sage	1 tsp
5 oz	Bitto or any fresh dairy cheese	150 g / 5 oz
1 tbsp	Grated parmesan cheese	1 tbsp
	Pepper	

1. Combine flours together and tip onto a pastry board. Make a well in the centre, break eggs into the middle with the milk, salt and a few drops of tepid water.

2. Knead ingredients well together to form a smooth dough, shape into a ball then wrap in transparent film or put in to a plastic bag and seal. Leave in a cool place for 30 minutes.

3. Roll the dough into a thickish rectangle, cut into strips ½ in / 1 cm wide by 1 in / 2.5 cm long.

4. Peel and dice potatoes. Bring a pan of salted water to the boil, add potatoes and beans to the pan and cook for about 10 minutes, then add the pizzoccheri pasta and cook a further 5 minutes. Drain vegetables and pasta, add butter, sage, chunks of bitto, parmesan and pepper.

5. Spoon onto a hot serving dish and put under a medium grill to melt cheese. Serve immediately.

Making Pasta
Sift the flour on to a board. Mix with some beaten egg, and salt. Knead together with floured hands

Add more beaten egg and knead again, continuing until all the eggs are added. Divide into small pieces, knead each piece, then re-shape all together to form a ball

Leave the dough to rest in a cool place for 30 minutes to 1 hour. Roll the dough out thinly and cut into noodles, lasagne or filled pasta shapes

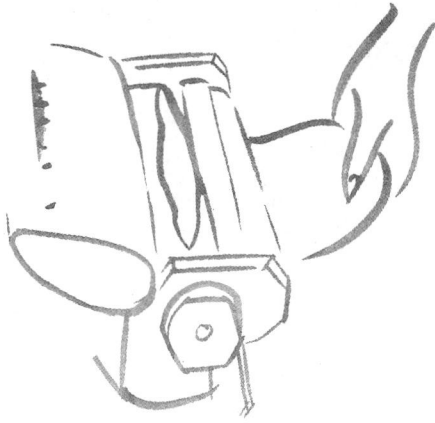

Alternatively, if you have a pasta machine, you can feed the rested and flattened dough into it

Roll a long, flat strip of pasta, taking care not to break the dough

If you enjoy making pasta it is well worth investing in a machine that will cut your pasta into different interesting shapes

Penne del pescatore 👨‍🍳

Fisherman's Penne

▭▬▷ 00:10   00:25 🍳

American	Ingredients	Metric/Imperial
1¾ lb	Fresh prawns	800 g / 1¾ lb

5
  or 14 oz can
	Tomatoes	5
		  or 400 g / 14 oz can

3 tbsp	Oil	2 tbsp
2 or 3	Bay leaves	2 or 3
	Salt and black pepper	

¾ lb	Penne pasta
	  (smooth, short-cut
	  pasta tubes)
		350 g / 12 oz

1 tbsp	Chopped parsley	1 tbsp

1. Plunge prawns into a pan of boiling salted water, cover, remove from the heat and leave to cool, then shell.
2. Peel and quarter tomatoes and remove seeds; if using canned tomatoes, use juice and fruit.
3. Heat oil in a large pan, add bay leaves, tomatoes and cook for 5-10 minutes, until mixture is reduced to a pulp.
4. Stir prawns gently into tomato sauce and season with salt and freshly ground black pepper. Leave to simmer over a low heat for 5 minutes.
5. Meanwhile cook penne pasta in plenty of boiling salted water until 'al dente'. Drain well.
6. Add the pasta to the prawn sauce over a medium heat and discard the bay leaves.
7. Spoon onto a hot serving dish, season with black pepper and garnish with chopped parsley.

Pasta alla potentina 👨‍🍳

Potentina Pasta

▭▬▷ 00:10   00:50 🍳

American	Ingredients	Metric/Imperial
6	Eggs	6
	Salt and pepper	
3 tbsp	Flour	2 tbsp
3 tbsp	White wine	2 tbsp
14 oz	Cooked fine macaroni	400 g / 14 oz
Scant ¼ cup	Oil	3 tbsp
1 tbsp	Butter	1 tbsp
1 tbsp	Bread crumbs	1 tbsp
¾ lb	Mozzarella cheese	350 g / 12 oz

1. Preheat oven to 400°F / 200°C / Gas Mark 6. Grease a large ovenproof serving dish.
2. Beat eggs with salt and pepper, add the flour, whisk well, and then the white wine. Mix in the macaroni.
3. Heat remaining oil in an iron frying pan. When just beginning to smoke, slide mixture into it, as for making normal omelette, cook for about 10 minutes, turn and cook the other side for 5 minutes. Place cooked omelette in dish, dot with butter, sprinkle with bread crumbs and cover with thin slices of mozzarella. Bake for about 25 minutes. Serve hot.

Pasta alla livornese
Leghorn-Style Pasta

	00:15		00:20	

American	Ingredients	Metric/Imperial
¼ lb	Lean raw ham	100 g / 4 oz
¼ lb	Neck of pork	100 g / 4 oz
1	Onion	1
Scant ¼ cup	Oil	3 tbsp
2	Garlic cloves	2
1	Bunch of basil	1
	Salt and pepper	
¼ tsp	Thyme	¼ tsp
¼ tsp	Paprika	¼ tsp
¼ cup	Best quality cognac	50 ml / 2 fl oz
14 oz	Semolina pasta	400 g / 14 oz

1. Chop ham and pork into small pieces. Peel and chop onion. Heat oil and fry meat and onion together with the crushed garlic, basil, thyme, paprika and cognac for 10 minutes, stirring from time to time. Add salt and freshly ground pepper.
2. Meanwhile cook pasta in boiling salted water until 'al dente', drain and stir into the meat sauce, mixing well.
3. Spoon on to a hot serving dish and serve immediately.

Pasta alla panna e funghi
Pasta with Cream Mushrooms

	00:15		00:15	

American	Ingredients	Metric/Imperial
½ lb	Mushrooms	225 g / 8 oz
	Salt and pepper	
1 tsp	Oil	1 tsp
14 oz	Pasta	400 g / 14 oz
1 cup	Whipping (double) cream	225 ml / 8 fl oz
1 tsp	Powdered truffle	1 tsp
	Nutmeg	
1 oz	Fontina or melting cheese	25 g / 1 oz
1	White truffle	1

1. Rinse mushrooms under hot water then remove stalks, slice tops and put into a bowl. Add salt, pepper and oil to mushrooms and leave to stand.
2. Put pasta to cook in boiling salted water until 'al dente'.
3. Meanwhile pour cream into a saucepan, add the truffle, the nutmeg and the mushrooms and leave to simmer for about 10 minutes. Slice cheese and white truffle thinly.
4. Drain pasta, mix in the cheese and spoon on to a serving dish. Cover with the mushroom sauce and garnish with slices of white truffle.

Pasta alla sbirraglia

Policeman's Pasta

⌦ 00:05   00:50 ⌫

American	Ingredients	Metric/Imperial
14 oz	Fresh lasagne	400 g / 14 oz
1 tsp	Cornstarch (cornflour)	1 tsp
½ cup	Whipping (double) cream	125 ml / 4 fl oz
½ cup	Cognac	125 ml / 4 fl oz
	Nutmeg	
	Salt and pepper	
1	Truffle	1
2 tbsp	Butter	25 g / 1 oz
1 tbsp	Grated cheese	1 tbsp

1. Preheat oven to 350°F / 180°C / Gas Mark 4. Grease an oblong ovenproof serving dish.
2. Cook lasagne a few pieces at a time in boiling salted water until 'al dente'. Drain and leave to dry on a clean tea towel or kitchen paper.
3. Meanwhile blend cornstarch with a little of the cream. Pour remaining cream into a saucepan, add blended cornstarch, cognac, nutmeg, pepper, salt and thinly sliced truffle, and bring to the boil stirring all the time. Simmer for 2 minutes.
4. Layer cooked lasagne in serving dish, add butter and pour over sauce. Sprinkle over grated cheese and bake in the oven for 25 minutes. Serve piping hot.

Pappardelle del cacciatore

Huntsman's Noodles

⌦ 00:10   00:30 ⌫

American	Ingredients	Metric/Imperial
½ lb	Mushrooms or dried mushrooms, softened	225 g / 8 oz
Scant ¼ cup	Olive oil	3 tbsp
1	Garlic clove	1
	Salt and pepper	
14 oz	Pappardelle	400 g / 14 oz
1 cup	Coffee (single) cream	225 ml / 8 fl oz
1 tbsp	Tomato sauce	1 tbsp
1 tbsp	Grated parmesan cheese	1 tbsp

1. Rinse fresh mushrooms under hot water then slice thinly. (Reconstitute dried mushrooms in water).
2. Heat oil in a pan, fry garlic for 1-2 minutes then remove. Add mushrooms to the pan and sauté for 2 minutes, then allow to simmer for about 20 minutes. Season with salt and pepper.
3. Meanwhile cook the pappardelle in boiling salted water until 'al dente', drain and put on a hot serving dish.
4. Add cream and tomato sauce to mushroom sauce, stir well then pour over pasta, sprinkle with the parmesan cheese.

Pappardelle con la lepre

Noodles with Hare

| | 00:20 | | 02:10 | |

American	Ingredients	Metric/Imperial
	Legs and back of a hare with liver and lights	
1	Onion	1
1	Garlic clove	1
Scant ¼ cup	Oil	3 tbsp
¼ tsp	Thyme	¼ tsp
¼ tsp	Sweet marjoram	¼ tsp
¼ tsp	Rosemary	¼ tsp
½ cup	Red wine (or more as required)	125 ml / 4 fl oz
1 cup	Meat stock	225 ml / 8 fl oz
¼ tsp	Nutmeg	¼ tsp
	Pepper	
14 oz	Pappardelle	400 g / 14 oz

1. Remove meat from the hare and cut into small pieces. Chop liver and lights and reserve.

2. Peel and chop onion, peel garlic. Heat half the oil in a large pan, fry onion, garlic, thyme, marjoram and rosemary together for 2-3 minutes.

3. Add hare meat to the pan and brown quickly. Pour over the wine and stock, bring to the boil, then reduce heat. Cover and simmer for about 2 hours.

4. Pour hare sauce into a blender and purée. Heat remaining oil in a pan and fry the prepared liver and lights together for 3-4 minutes. Pour hare purée into pan and mix ingredients together. Add nutmeg and pepper.

5. Cook pappardelle in boiling salted water until 'al dente', drain and stir into hare sauce.

6. Spoon on to a heated serving dish and serve.

Pasta e ricotta sprint

Pasta with Two Cheeses

	00:05		00:15	

American	Ingredients	Metric/Imperial
½ lb	Very fresh ricotta cheese	25 g / 8 oz
½ cup	Coffee (single) cream	100 ml / 3½ fl oz
4 tbsp	Butter	50 g / 2 oz
	Pepper	
3 tbsp	Grated parmesan cheese	2 tbsp
14 oz	Pasta	400 g / 14 oz
1 tsp	Grated parmesan cheese	1 tsp
1 tsp	Grated pecorino cheese	1 tsp

1. Sieve ricotta into a saucepan. Stir in cream with butter, season with pepper and add parmesan. Heat gently over a low heat. Do not allow to boil.
2. Cook pasta in boiling salted water until 'al dente', drain and tip into the ricotta sauce.
3. Spoon onto a heated serving dish, mix together the teaspoon of parmesan and pecorino cheeses and sprinkle over the top.

Maccheroni Trinacria al forno

Sicilian Baked Macaroni

	00:45		01:00	

American	Ingredients	Metric/Imperial
2	Large eggplant (aubergines)	2
	Salt and pepper	
2	Garlic cloves	2
14 oz can	Tomatoes	400 g / 14 oz can
⅔ cup	Oil	150 ml / ¼ pint
14 oz	Pilchards	400 g / 14 oz
¾ lb	Macaroni	350 g / 12 oz
	Oregano	
½ cup	Grated cheese	50 g / 2 oz
1 tbsp	Butter	1 tbsp

1. Preheat oven to 350°F / 180°C / Gas Mark 4. Grease an ovenproof serving dish.
2. Slice eggplant thinly, place in a colander and sprinkle with salt. Leave for 30 minutes, then rinse under cold water and dry well.
3. Peel garlic and chop finely. Heat 1 tablespoon of the oil in a large saucepan and add garlic and fry gently until golden. Add tomatoes and juice from can. Season with salt and pepper and simmer for 15 minutes.
4. Meanwhile clean pilchards. Slit to open but leave halves joined, wash under cold running water and add to sauce. Cover and leave to cook a further 10 minutes.
5. Heat remaining oil in a large pan and fry slices of eggplant until lightly browned, then drain on kitchen paper.
6. Cook macaroni in boiling salted water until 'al dente', drain and add a dash of oil to prevent it sticking together. Arrange

pasta on the base of the dish, top with pilchard sauce, then the eggplant.

7. Add freshly ground pepper and oregano to grated cheese and scatter dabs of butter over surface. Bake for about 30 minutes until lightly browned. Serve piping hot.

Maccheroni alla siciliana

Sicilian-Style Macaroni

00:10   00:25

American	Ingredients	Metric/Imperial
1	Small onion	1
½	Sweet pepper	½
1	Garlic clove	1
Scant ¼ cup	Oil	3 tbsp
1	Bay leaf	1
Scant ¼ cup	Tomato purée	3 tbsp
8	Black olives	8
½ tsp	Anchovy paste	½ tsp
¼ tsp	Oregano	¼ tsp
¼ tsp	Basil	¼ tsp
	Salt and pepper	
½ lb	Fine macaroni	225 g / 8 oz
¼ cup	Grated pecorino cheese	25 g / 1 oz

1. Chop onion and sweet pepper, peel garlic. Heat oil in a pan and sauté these with a bay leaf for 3 minutes.

2. Add tomato purée, black olives, anchovy paste, oregano and basil. Season with salt and pepper, cover and cook over a low heat for 8-10 minutes.

3. Cook macaroni in boiling salted water until 'al dente', drain and add to the sauce, stirring both ingredients carefully until thoroughly mixed. Sprinkle with fresh pepper and grated pecorino and serve immediately.

Pasta alla cipolla

Onion Pasta

00:10   00:25

American	Ingredients	Metric/Imperial
2	Large onions	2
¼ cup	Butter	50 g / 2 oz
	Salt	
2	Eggs	2
14 oz	Bavette (thin noodles)	400 g / 14 oz
1 tbsp	Grated parmesan cheese	1 tbsp

1. Peel and thinly slice onions. Melt butter and cook onions slowly for about 10 minutes until soft without browning, then remove from the heat.

2. Add salt and beaten eggs to the pan and mix ingredients thoroughly.

3. Cook bavette in boiling salted water until 'al dente', drain, add the onion sauce and top with grated cheese.

Maccheroni di primavera

Springtime Macaroni

	00:15		00:50	

American	Ingredients	Metric/Imperial
2 lb	Asparagus or frozen packets of asparagus	1 kg / 2 lb
½ cup	Butter	100 g / 4 oz
¾ lb	Roman ricotta or piedmontese cheese	350 g / 12 oz
¼ cup	Milk	50 ml / 2 fl oz
	Salt and pepper	
14 oz	Macaroni	400 g / 14 oz
¼ cup	Grated parmesan cheese	25 g / 1 oz
2	Eggs	2
¼ tsp	Nutmeg	¼ tsp
3 tbsp	Grated cheese	2 tbsp

1. Preheat oven to 375°F / 190°C / Gas Mark 5. Grease an ovenproof serving dish.
2. Clean asparagus and cook for 5 minutes in boiling salted water, drain well. Cut into small pieces discarding hard stems.
3. In a large pan, melt a quarter of the butter add asparagus and cook until golden.
4. In a bowl beat ricotta with the milk, salt and pepper to obtain a smooth cream.
5. Cook macaroni until 'al dente', then drain. Add the rest of the butter and parmesan to the pasta, and spoon over the base of the dish.
6. Top with the asparagus and half the ricotta. Continue layering in this way finishing with a layer of macaroni.
7. Beat eggs with salt, pepper, nutmeg and grated cheese and pour over macaroni. Bake for 30 minutes until golden. Serve piping hot.

Maccheroni alla vodka

Macaroni with Vodka

| | 00:05 | | 00:30 | |

American	Ingredients	Metric/Imperial
1	Large onion	1
1 oz	Sausage	25 g / 1 oz
3 tbsp	Butter	2 tbsp
½ cup	Vodka	125 ml / 4 fl oz
2 cups	Whipping (double) cream	450 ml / 16 fl oz
	Salt and pepper	
14 oz	Macaroni	400 g / 14 oz

1. Peel and chop onion, skin sausage and slice into small pieces.
2. Melt butter and cook the onion and sausage for about 5 minutes over a medium heat. Pour over three-quarters of vodka and bring to the boil. Reduce heat and simmer for 8-10 minutes. Finally stir in all but 2 tablespoons [25 ml / 1 fl oz] of the cream, simmer for a further 3-5 minutes, then season.
3. Boil macaroni in salted water until 'al dente', drain and stir into the vodka cream sauce.
4. Spoon onto a large serving plate, pour over the remaining vodka and cream and serve immediately.

Corzetti alla rivierasca

Coastal-Style Corzetti

| | 00:30 | | 00:45 | |

American	Ingredients	Metric/Imperial
1 (½ lb)	Fresh salmon slice	1 (225 g / 8 oz)
Scant ¼ cup	Oil	3 tbsp
1	Onion	1
½ cup	Dry white wine	125 ml / 4 fl oz
½ cup	Stock	125 ml / 4 fl oz
5 tbsp	Tomato purée	4 tbsp
1 tsp	Fresh, chopped basil	1 tsp
2	Walnuts	2
14 oz	Corzetti (spiral pasta shapes)	400 g / 14 oz
	Salt	

1. Cut the fresh salmon into thin strips.
2. Heat the oil, add the chopped onion, cook for 4 minutes then add the salmon strips. Cook for about 10 minutes, add the white wine, the stock and the tomato purée, allow to simmer over a very low heat, so that the sauce remains very thick.
3. Pass through the blender. Chop the fresh basil and walnuts finely, retain a quarter for the garnish and mix the rest with the sauce.
4. Heat a saucepan with plenty of salted water and when it boils cook the corzetti. Drain, season at once with the fish sauce and serve hot. Add extra chopped basil and walnuts sprinkled on top.

Maccheroni alla chitarra

Guitar Macaroni

◁▭▭ 00:35   00:25 ▭

American	Ingredients	Metric/Imperial
¼ lb	Bacon	100 g / 4 oz
Scant ¼ cup	Oil	3 tbsp
1	Sweet red pepper	1
6	Tomatoes, peeled	6
3 cups	Flour	350 g / 12 oz
4	Eggs	4
	Salt and pepper	

1. Cube the bacon, heat oil in a pan and cook bacon for 2 minutes. Add chopped sweet pepper and tomatoes, stir with a wooden spoon and cook over a low heat until of a thickish consistency.
2. Sift flour onto a pastry board, make a well in the centre and tip in beaten eggs to obtain a firm dough and draw out with a rolling-pin over a guitar (a frame on which wires are stretched) to obtain thin strips of pasta, or cut into thin strips.
3. Cook these in plenty of boiling salted water until 'al dente'. Drain, season with hot sauce and serve.

Bigoli con sardelle

Bigoli with Sardines

This is a typical Lombard recipe.

◁▭▭ 00:20   00:20 ▭

American	Ingredients	Metric/Imperial
¼ lb	Sardines	100 g / 4 oz
14 oz	Bigoli pasta	400 g / 14 oz
	Salt	
3 tbsp	Olive oil	2 tbsp
2	Garlic cloves	2

1. Clean, bone and wash the fish and place them on a board.
2. Cook the bigoli pasta in a large saucepan with plenty of salted water.
3. Heat the oil, add the garlic, and when the garlic turns golden, put in the sardines. While they are cooking squash them with a wooden fork without frying them.
4. Drain the bigoli when firm to the bite and put them in an earthenware dish, pour over the fish sauce and serve very hot.

Pasta e bisi

Pasta and Peas

	00:10		00:25	

American	Ingredients	Metric/Imperial
2 ¼ cups	Small new peas, or frozen peas	350 g / 12 oz
½ cup	Butter	100 g / 4 oz
½ lb	Chicken livers	225 g / 8 oz
2	Sage leaves	2
14 oz	Pasta	400 g / 14 oz
1 tbsp	Grated parmesan cheese	1 tbsp
	Cognac (optional)	

1. Boil peas for 10 minutes then drain. Melt butter in a frying pan, add peas and washed chopped chicken livers and brown slightly, stirring frequently. Add sage leaves, and continue cooking a further 5 minutes.
2. Bring a large saucepan of salted water to the boil, add chosen pasta and cook until 'al dente'.
3. Drain and sprinkle with grated parmesan, then stir in the chicken liver sauce. Add a little cognac if desired and serve.

Pasta alla toscana

Tuscan-Style Pasta

	00:10		01:10	

American	Ingredients	Metric/Imperial
1	Onion	1
1	Sweet yellow pepper	1
1	Carrot	1
1	Celery stalk	1
2 oz	Bacon	50 g / 2 oz
	Oil	
2	Garlic cloves	2
¾ lb	Tomato purée	350 g / 12 oz
1	Bunch of basil	1
½ cup	Dry white wine	125 ml / 4 fl oz
1 oz	Capers	25 g / 1 oz
	Pepper	
¼ tsp	Oregano	¼ tsp
14 oz	Spaghetti	400 g / 14 oz
¼ cup	Grated pecorino cheese	25 g / 1 oz

1. Peel and chop onion, sweet yellow pepper, carrot and celery. Dice bacon. Heat oil in a saucepan and cook prepared vegetables, bacon, garlic, tomato purée and basil for 5 minutes. Pour over the wine and simmer over a low heat for about 1 hour. Add capers, pepper and oregano 5 minutes before the end of cooking time.
2. Cook spaghetti in plenty of boiling salted water until 'al dente', drain and mix pasta into vegetable mixture.
3. Spoon onto a serving dish and sprinkle over the grated cheese. Serve immediately.

Maccheroni gratinati

Macaroni au Gratin

| | 00:15 | 01:05 | |

American	Ingredients	Metric/Imperial
5 oz	Thick slice of cooked ham	150 g / 5 oz
7 oz	Mushrooms	200 g / 7 oz
14 oz can	Peeled tomatoes	400 g / 14 oz can
2	Garlic cloves	2
Scant ¼ cup	Oil	3 tbsp
	Salt and pepper	
14 oz	Macaroni	400 g / 14 oz
3 tbsp	Cornstarch (cornflour)	2 tbsp
1¼ cups	Milk	300 ml / ½ pint
3 tbsp	Butter	2 tbsp
¼ tsp	Nutmeg	¼ tsp
1 tbsp	Grated cheese	1 tbsp

1. Preheat oven to 350°F / 180°C / Gas Mark 4. Grease an oblong serving dish.
2. Dice ham, wash mushrooms and slice, peel tomatoes and roughly chop. Peel garlic.
3. In a large frying pan, heat oil and cook mushrooms and crushed garlic for 1-2 minutes, stirring all the time. Add ham, season with salt and pepper and cook for a few minutes.
4. Add tomatoes to the pan, cover and simmer for 10 minutes.
5. Meanwhile cook macaroni in plenty of boiling salted water until 'al dente', drain and rinse under cold water, then stir into the tomato sauce.
6. Make a sauce by blending cornstarch with a little milk, add remainder of milk and heat in a pan until boiling, stirring all the time. Add half the butter, salt, pepper and nutmeg.
7. Spoon the macaroni and tomato sauce over the base of the serving dish, cover with the white sauce, sprinkle with grated cheese and scatter remaining butter in knobs over the top.
8. Bake for 35-40 minutes until golden and serve hot.

Spaghetti al cartoccio

Spaghetti in Foil

| | 00:15 | 00:15 | |

American	Ingredients	Metric/Imperial
1¼ lb	Shellfish (mussels, clams, limpets) weighed with the shell	600 g / 1¼ lb
⅓ cup	Vegetable oil	5 tbsp
2	Garlic cloves	2
1	Bunch of parsley	1
Scant ¼ cup	Chopped tomatoes	3 tbsp
14 oz	Spaghetti	400 g / 14 oz
	Salt and pepper	
	Aluminium foil	

1. Preheat oven to 400°F / 200°C / Gas Mark 6.
2. Clean shell fish thoroughly. Heat oil in a frying pan, and

when very hot, add shellfish, garlic, chopped parsley, and chopped tomatoes. Cook for 5 minutes, stirring all the time, then leave sauce to thicken over a low heat.

3. Half cook spaghetti in boiling salted water, then drain and pass under running cold water. Stir into shellfish sauce, mixing well.

4. Spread a big sheet of aluminum foil over a baking sheet. In the centre place the seasoned spaghetti, sprinkle the top with a thin trickle of oil, add pepper and close up the foil, leaving a fairly large space above, so that the steam may circulate inside.

5. Bake in the oven for 10 minutes, then serve parcel of spaghetti at the table.

Note: the shellfish may be cooked with or without valves.

Spaghetti all'arrabbiata

Arrabbiata-Style Spaghetti

00:30   00:20

American	Ingredients	Metric/Imperial
14 oz	Chitterlings mixed with pork	400 g / 14 oz
10	Shelled walnuts	10
½ cup	Vegetable oil	125 ml / 4 fl oz
4	Garlic cloves	4
¼ tsp	Red paprika	¼ tsp
	Salt and pepper	
⅓ cup	Raisins	50 g / 2 oz
14 oz	Spaghetti	400 g / 14 oz
1 tbsp	Grated pecorino cheese	1 tbsp

1. Clean chitterlings and chop, blend walnuts to a purée with a little of the oil. Heat remaining oil in a frying pan and when very hot fry chopped chitterlings with pork, crushed garlic, red paprika and pepper for 5 minutes.

2. Blanch raisins, drain and add to pan with walnut purée and wine. Stir well then purée sauce in a food processor or blender, return to pan and leave over a very low heat.

3. Meanwhile cook spaghetti in plenty of boiling salted water until 'al dente' and drain.

4. Stir grated pecorino into spaghetti and then mix pasta and cheese into sauce in frying pan and continue to cook over a low heat for 5 minutes.

5. Spoon onto a hot serving dish, sprinkle over fresh pepper and serve hot.

Spaghetti alla creola

Creole-Style Spaghetti

⌐▭▭ 🔪   00:15   00:45 ⌐▱

American	Ingredients	Metric/Imperial
1 lb	Fresh or frozen scampi and shrimps, without shells	500 g / 1 lb
3 tbsp	Vegetable oil	2 tbsp
7 oz	Tomato pulp	200 g / 7 oz
1 tsp	Pepper	1 tsp
2 tsp	Curry powder	2 tsp
½ cup	Bourbon	125 ml / 4 fl oz
14 oz	Spaghetti	400 g / 14 oz
	Salt	
1 cup	Coffee (single) cream	225 ml / 8 fl oz
1 tbsp	Grated cheese	1 tbsp

1. Thoroughly clean fresh shrimps and scampi and remove shells. Heat oil and when very hot quickly fry prepared fish with tomato pulp for 5 minutes, stirring all the time. Season, add curry powder and pour over the bourbon. Cover and simmer for about 30 minutes.
2. Cook spaghetti in boiling salted water until 'al dente', drain and stir in cream and cheese, then pour over fish sauce and serve.

Variations: lobster, sea crab or abalone may be substituted for shrimps and scampi in this recipe.

Spaghetti ai frutti di mare

Seafood Spaghetti

⌐▭▭▷   00:05   00:20 ⌐▱

American	Ingredients	Metric/Imperial
½ lb	Frozen shellfish, without shells	225 g / 8 oz
2	Plum tomatoes, ripe or pulped	2
2	Garlic cloves	2
Scant ¼ cup	Vegetable oil	3 tbsp
1	Bunch of basil	1
	Salt and pepper	
14 oz	Fine spaghetti	400 g / 14 oz
1 tbsp	Grated pecorino cheese	1 tbsp

1. Put shellfish in a pan with tomato, garlic, half of the oil, basil, salt and plenty of pepper. Cover and simmer for 20 minutes.
2. Meanwhile cook pasta in boiling salted water with the rest of the oil, until 'al dente'. Drain and put in a serving bowl, sprinkle over the pecorino and pour over shellfish sauce. Serve immediately.

Conchiglie ai cavolini di Bruxelles

Pasta Shells with Brussels Sprouts

	00:20		00:30	

American	Ingredients	Metric/Imperial
¼ cup	Butter	50 g / 2 oz
2 oz	Bacon	50 g / 2 oz
1	Garlic clove	1
1 lb	Brussels sprouts	500 g / 1 lb
½ lb	Peeled tomatoes	225 g / 8 oz
1 tsp	Chopped basil	1 tsp
	Salt	
1 lb	Shell-shaped pasta	450 g / 1 lb
1 tbsp	Grated parmesan cheese	1 tbsp

1. In a large pan, heat the butter, add the bacon chopped into cubes. Add a clove of crushed garlic.
2. Wash and dry the brussels sprouts, mix with the bacon and garlic and allow to absorb the flavor for about 15 minutes, then add the chopped peeled tomatoes, some chopped basil and stir. Continue cooking for a further 15 minutes.
3. Heat plenty of salted water, boil the pasta shells until firm to the bite. Drain, keep a little of the cooking liquid and add the sprouts immediately.
4. Mix in two or three spoonfuls of cooking liquid, sprinkle with plenty of grated cheese and serve piping hot.

Cook's tip: If there should be any left over, this pasta is also excellent heated in the oven with half a cup of béchamel sauce mixed with it. Place the pasta and béchamel in an ovenproof dish and reheat in a moderate oven.

Spaghetti alle vongole

Spaghetti with Clams

	00:20		00:20	

American	Ingredients	Metric/Imperial
1 ¼ lb	Clams	600 g / 1 ¼ lb
Scant ¼ cup	Vegetable oil	3 tbsp
6	Sprigs of parsley	6
14 oz can	Peeled tomatoes	400 g / 14 oz can
	Salt and pepper	
1 ¼ lb	Spaghetti	600 g / 1 ¼ lb

1. Wash clams in several changes of water until water remains clear, then wipe dry. Heat oil in a pan, add clams, cover and cook for 5 - 8 minutes until shells open, discarding any that remain closed.
2. Add the parsley and the tomatoes to the pan and cook for a further 7 minutes. Taste and adjust seasoning.
3. Cook spaghetti in plenty of boiling salted water until 'al dente', drain and spoon onto a hot serving dish. Pour over clam sauce and serve immediately.

Fusilli alla napoletana

Neapolitan-Style Fusilli

This recipe is very ancient and famous throughout Campania.

00:30   01:25

American	Ingredients	Metric/Imperial
½ cup	Oil	125 ml / 4 fl oz
1	Onion	1
1	Celery stalk	1
1	Carrot	1
2	Garlic cloves	2
¼ lb	Neapolitan spicy salami	100 g / 4 oz
¾ lb	Ground (minced) lamb or pork	350 g / 12 oz
½ cup	Dry white wine	125 ml / 4 fl oz
½ lb	Ricotta cheese	225 g / 8 oz
	Salt and freshly ground black pepper	
½ tsp	Hot paprika	½ tsp
5 tbsp	Tomato purée or sauce	4 tbsp
14 oz	Fusilli (spiral-shaped pasta)	400 g / 14 oz

1. Heat the oil in a frying pan over a low heat. Prepare the vegetables. Chop the onion, slice celery, dice the carrot and crush the cloves of garlic.
2. Chop bacon and chop salami. Add to pan with vegetables and ground (minced) meat. Mix well and brown over a medium heat moistening a little at a time with dry white wine.
3. Crumble the ricotta into the sauce, mix and season with salt, pepper and hot paprika.
4. Add tomato purée to the meat sauce and continue cooking for 1 hour.
5. Heat a saucepan containing plenty of salted water and, when boiling, toss in the fusilli. Cook until 'al dente' and drain. Season at once with the sauce.

Spaghetti alla barese

Bari-Style Spaghetti

00:10   00:10

American	Ingredients	Metric/Imperial
2 lb	Turnip tops	1 kg / 2 lb
1 lb	Large spaghetti	450 g / 1 lb
3 tbsp	Vegetable oil	2 tbsp
2	Garlic cloves	2
½ lb	Tomato purée	225 g / 8 oz
1	Bunch of basil	1

1. Trim turnip tops, retaining tip and using remainder of green part for minestrone.
2. Cook turnip tops and spaghetti in a large pan of boiling salted water for 8-10 minutes, until pasta is 'al dente'.

3. Meanwhile heat oil in a pan, and when very hot fry the garlic for 1-2 minutes. Add tomato purée and chopped basil, stir well and remove from heat.

4. Drain pasta and turnip tops, stir in tomato sauce and spoon onto a hot serving dish. Serve immediately.

Fusilli grande estate

High Summer Fusilli

00:25
plus 00:30 in refrigerator

00:25

American	Ingredients	Metric/Imperial
½ lb	Frozen or shelled fresh peas	225 g / 8 oz
1 ⅓ cups	Shelled, cooked prawns	225 g / 8 oz
2	Ripe but firm pear-shaped tomatoes	2
3 tbsp	Pickled capers	2 tbsp
7 oz can	Tuna	200 g / 7 oz can
Scant ¼ cup	Oil	3 tbsp
1	Lemon	1
½ lb	Fusilli pasta	225 g / 8 oz
	Salt and pepper	
¼ tsp	Oregano	¼ tsp

1. Cook the frozen or fresh peas, drain and place into an earthenware dish.

2. Cut the prawns in half and add them to the peas.

3. Plunge the tomatoes into boiling water, skin them, remove their seeds and cut into small pieces. Add the tomatoes to the other ingredients with pickled capers.

4. Drain the oil from a small can of tuna fish, break it up with a fork and then add it to the dish, mixing gently. Season with oil and the juice of a lemon.

5. Cook the fusilli in plenty of boiling salted water, drain and pass under cold water. Drain well and season with a small amount of oil. Allow to cool.

6. Mix the pasta with the other ingredients, add pepper, salt and sprinkle with oregano. Cover and chill in the refrigerator for about 30 minutes before serving.

Bucatini alla gaetana

Gaeta-Style Bucatini

This is a typical recipe of Gaeta and dates back to the time of wild boar hunting in southern Italy.

	00:20		00:20

American	Ingredients	Metric/Imperial
14 oz	Young wild pig meat or pork	400 g / 14 oz
Scant ¼ cup	Oil	3 tbsp
1	Onion	1
2 or 3	Mint leaves	2 or 3
1	Garlic clove	1
½ lb	Green olives	225 g / 8 oz
½ cup	Dry white wine	125 ml / 4 fl oz
¼ lb	Wild boar or calf's liver	100 g / 4 oz
Scant ¼ cup	Stock	3 tbsp
14 oz	Bucatini pasta	400 g / 14 oz
	Salt	
1 tbsp	Pecorino (ewe's milk cheese)	1 tbsp
¼ tsp	Oregano	¼ tsp

1. Finely chop the pork. Heat the oil in a frying pan, and brown the meat. Lower the heat and add the finely chopped onion, mint leaves and crushed garlic. Cook for 5 minutes.

2. Mix well, add the green olives and white wine.

3. Chop the liver into small pieces and add to the sauce with the stock. Allow to simmer for 10 minutes.

4. Cook the pasta in boiling salted water until 'al dente', drain and toss it with the pecorino and oregano. Mix with the sauce and serve.

Pasta con ragù al tonno

Pasta with Tuna Sauce

⌦ 00:10   00:40 ⌫

American	Ingredients	Metric/Imperial
1	Onion	1
1	Garlic clove	1
3	Anchovies in oil	3
¼ lb	Tuna fish in oil	100 g / 4 oz
3 tbsp	Olive oil	2 tbsp
¼ cup	Butter	50 g / 2 oz
½ lb	Peeled tomatoes	225 g / 8 oz
2 or 3	Basil leaves	2 or 3
	Salt and pepper	
¾ lb	Pasta (sedani rigati)	350 g / 12 oz

1. Peel and finely chop onion and garlic. Pound anchovies to a pulp and break up tuna fish and stir into anchovies with half of the oil.
2. Heat oil and butter together in a pan and when foaming sauté onion and garlic for 2-3 minutes. Add peeled tomatoes, basil, salt and pepper and pounded fish. Cook for 2-3 minutes, stirring all the time, cover and allow to simmer over a low heat for 30 minutes.
3. Cook pasta in boiling salted water until 'al dente', drain and stir into tuna sauce.
4. Spoon onto a hot serving dish and serve immediately.

Maccheroni con la piovra

Macaroni with Octopus

⌦ 00:10   00:40 ⌫

American	Ingredients	Metric/Imperial
1 ¼ lb	Octopus	600 g / 1 ¼ lb
2	Bay leaves	2
Scant ¼ cup	Oil	3 tbsp
3	Garlic cloves	3
3 tbsp	Chopped parsley	2 tbsp
14 oz	Macaroni	400 g / 14 oz
	Salt	

1. Clean octopus thoroughly, beat and put in a saucepan, with plenty of water; do not add salt. Add bay leaves, bring to the boil and cook until the octopus becomes red, drain and cool.
2. In a frying pan heat oil, peel and crush 2 cloves of garlic, add to the pan with most of the chopped parsley.
3. Cut octopus into small pieces, add to the pan, stirring for about 10 minutes.
4. Meanwhile boil macaroni until 'al dente' in plenty of lightly salted water, drain well and stir into the octopus and its cooking juices, until thoroughly mixed.
5. Spoon onto a hot serving dish and garnish with chopped parsley and crushed garlic.

Pasta con le verdure piccanti

Pasta with Spicy Vegetables

	00:10	00:25

American	Ingredients	Metric/Imperial
2	Sweet yellow peppers	2
1	Onion	1
Scant ¼ cup	Vegetable oil	3 tbsp
1 ½ cups	Spinach, boiled and squeezed	350 g / 12 oz
2	Garlic cloves	2
1	Bunch of basil	1
½ tsp	Red paprika	½ tsp
	Pepper	
1 cup	Dry white wine	225 ml / 8 fl oz
¾ lb	Pasta	350 g / 12 oz
	Grated pecorino cheese	

1. Deseed and slice peppers, peel and chop onion.
2. Heat oil and add the cooked spinach and garlic and sauté for 5 minutes stirring all the time. Add peppers, onion and basil to pan and cook for a further 2 minutes.
3. Finally stir in paprika, pepper and white wine. Cover and simmer for 10 minutes.
4. Meanwhile cook pasta in boiling salted water until 'al dente'. Drain and stir into vegetable sauce.
5. Spoon onto a hot serving dish, sprinkle a little oil over surface and grated pecorino and serve at once.

Pasta con le sarde

Pasta with Sardines

	00:30	00:45

American	Ingredients	Metric/Imperial
1	Head of wild fennel	1
2	Onions	2
14 oz	Sardines	400 g / 14 oz
4	Anchovies	4
Scant ¼ cup	Vegetable oil	3 tbsp
2 oz	Pine kernels	50 g / 2 oz
⅓ cup	Sultanas	50 g / 2oz
	Salt	
1 lb	Macaroni	450 g / 1 lb

1. Preheat oven to 350°F / 180°C / Gas Mark 4. Grease an oblong ovenproof serving dish.
2. Trim and thinly slice the fennel, cook in boiling salted water for 10 minutes, drain. Peel and chop onions, clean and pound sardines, clean and bone anchovies.
3. Heat the oil in a large pan, add the onions and cook for 2-3 minutes. Add fennel, half the sardines and anchovies to pan. Cook for 3 minutes stirring all the time, add pine nuts, sultanas

and ⅔ cup [150 ml / ¼ pint] of vegetable water to the pan, cover and simmer over a low heat for 10 minutes.

4. Put the remaining sardines in a bowl and add salt and oil. Leave to stand. Cook macaroni in boiling salted water until 'al dente'.

5. Drain and spoon half the cooked pasta over the base of the serving dish. Mix the remaining macaroni with half the fennel sauce. Spoon the sardines over the pasta then top with the mixed pasta and sauce.

6. Bake for 20 minutes and serve with a crunchy salad.

Conchiglie alla spagnola

Spanish-Style Shells

00:30   01:15

American	Ingredients	Metric/Imperial
4 tbsp	Butter	50 g / 2 oz
Scant ¼ cup	Oil	3 tbsp
2	Onions	2
2	Carrots	2
1	Celery stalk	1
1 lb	Lean veal pieces	500 g / 1 lb
3 tbsp	Flour	2 tbsp
¼ cup	White wine	50 ml / 2 fl oz
1 cup	Stock	225 ml / 8 fl oz
½ lb	Peeled tomatoes	225 g / 8 oz
2	Large sweet peppers	2
1 tsp	Oregano	1 tsp
	Salt and pepper	
¾ lb	Durum wheat shells	350 g / 12 oz
½ lb	Mozzarella cheese	225 g / 8 oz

1. Preheat the oven to 400°F / 200°C /Gas Mark 6.

2. Heat half the butter and oil in a frying pan, add thinly sliced onions, carrots and celery, cook over a medium heat.

3. Push the vegetables to one side after 5 minutes.

4. Cut the veal into small pieces, toss in flour and add to the pan and fry on both sides until brown.

5. Sprinkle with white wine and when it has evaporated, continue the cooking moistening with stock, with the lid on the pan. Stir occasionally and after 10 minutes add 2 peeled and squashed tomatoes.

6. In a separate pan, heat remaining oil and butter and lightly fry a large diced onion. When the onion becomes transparent, add the deseeded sweet peppers which have been cut into fairly small slices, and the peeled tomatoes, season with salt and pepper, sprinkle with oregano and leave to cook. After 20 minutes add the onion and sweet pepper sauce to the meat mixture, mix well and adjust seasoning. Continue cooking until pasta is ready.

7. Cook the shells in plenty of salted and boiling water. Drain the pasta, mix with meat mixture, and sauce. Turn into an ovenproof dish, sprinkle the surface with oregano and mozzarella cut into small pieces. Place in hot oven for 15 minutes and serve immediately.

Bucatini alla brava

Dashing Bucatini

00:20   00:30

American	Ingredients	Metric/Imperial
¼ cup	Butter	50 g / 2 oz
1	Onion	1
1 cup	Cooked prawns	175 g / 6 oz
½ cup	Whipping (double) cream	125 ml / 4 fl oz
¼ tsp	Chopped thyme	¼ tsp
¼ tsp	Chopped sweet marjoram	¼ tsp
1 tsp	Curry powder	1 tsp
1 tsp	Fine-grain semolina	1 tsp
	Salt	
14 oz	Bucatini pasta	400 g / 14 oz

1. In a small saucepan, melt the butter, add the finely chopped onion, the peeled prawns, cream, thyme, marjoram and the curry powder, mix well over a low heat.
2. Sprinkle on the semolina, keeping the heat low and mixing carefully.
3. Heat plenty of salted water in a large saucepan, when it boils toss in the bucatini pasta stirring frequently. When cooking is completed, drain and season at once with the sauce. Cheese is not necessary. You may use other types of pasta, from macaroni to spaghetti, according to taste.

Penne con le zucchine crude

Penne with Raw Gourds

00:15   00:15

American	Ingredients	Metric/Imperial
4	Coastal gourds	4
¼ cup	Refined lard	50 g / 2 oz
2	Garlic cloves	2
⅔ cup	Ripe black olives	100 g / 4 oz
1 lb	Penne pasta	450 g / 1 lb
	Salt and pepper	

1. Wash gourds carefully and slice finely.
2. Heat lard until hot, add the crushed cloves of garlic and cook for 1-2 minutes, then add black olives and cook for a further 2 minutes, stirring all the time.
3. Cook pasta in boiling salted water until 'al dente', then drain and add olive sauce to pasta and stir in the gourds. Season with pepper and serve immediately.

Pasticcio alla Bambi

Bambi-Style Pie

| | 00:15 | | 00:55 | |

American	Ingredients	Metric/Imperial
3 cups	Béchamel sauce	700 ml / 1 ¼ pints
3 tbsp	Grated parmesan cheese	2 tbsp
⅓ cup	Butter	75 g / 3 oz
1 ½ oz	Dried mushrooms	40 g / 1 ½ oz
14 oz	Canned peas	400 g / 14 oz
7 oz	Fontina cheese	200 g / 7 oz
2 oz	Slice of cooked ham	50 g / 2 oz
1 lb	Conchiglioni (large shell-shaped pasta)	450 g / 1 lb
¼ cup	Butter	50 g / 2 oz

1. Preheat oven to 350°F / 180°C / Gas Mark 4. Grease an oblong ovenproof serving dish.
2. Make béchamel sauce and stir in half the grated parmesan.
3. Heat the butter, sauté the mushrooms and the drained peas for 3 minutes. Cut the fontina and the ham into small pieces and put in a bowl. Add the cooked mushrooms and the peas and mix well.
4. Cook conchiglioni in plenty of boiling salted water until 'al dente', drain and spoon half the pasta over base of dish. Top with half the mushroom sauce then a layer of béchamel. Continue to layer remaining pasta sauce and béchamel. Sprinkle over remaining parmesan, add dabs of butter and bake for 30 minutes until golden brown.

Pasta con la ricotta

Pasta with Ricotta

| | 00:10 | | 00:10 | |

American	Ingredients	Metric/Imperial
7 oz	Ricotta cheese	200 g / 7 oz
1 cup	Whipping (double) cream	225 ml / 8 fl oz
	Salt and pepper	
¼ tsp	Paprika	¼ tsp
1 tbsp	Sugar	1 tbsp
1 tbsp	Cinnamon	1 tbsp
14 oz	Hard-grain semolina pasta, e.g. spaghetti, macaroni, zite, or rigatoni	400 g / 14 oz

1. In a bowl mix the ricotta with cream, pepper, salt, paprika, sugar and cinnamon.
2. In a large saucepan cook the pasta till 'al dente', in plenty of salted water. Drain well and stir in the ricotta sauce over a low heat, then serve.

Variations: other cheeses may be used such as romand or piedmont ricotta, ligurian curd cheese or strong apulian ricotta.

Pasta alla veneziana

Venetian-Style Pasta

| | 00:15 | | 00:50 | |

American	Ingredients	Metric/Imperial
1 ¼ lb	Well-filleted fish in a slice or whole	600 g / 1 ¼ lb
1	Onion	1
⅓ cup	Butter	65 g / 2 ½ oz
3 tbsp	White wine	2 tbsp
5 tbsp	Tomato concentrate	4 tbsp
¼ lb	Pine kernels	100 g / 4 oz
1 cup	Béchamel sauce	225 ml / 8 fl oz
1 tbsp	Grated parmesan cheese	1 tbsp
14 oz	Spaghetti	400 g / 14 oz
	Bread crumbs as required	
	Salt	

1. Preheat the oven to 400°F / 200°C / Gas Mark 6. Grease an ovenproof dish.
2. Poach fish in simmering water for about 10 minutes, then drain, and chop up flesh into bite-size pieces. Peel and finely chop onion.
3. Melt half the butter in a pan and when foaming add onion and fish and sauté for 2 minutes. Add white wine, tomato concentrate, pine kernels. Simmer for 5 minutes, uncovered.
4. Prepare a béchamel sauce with the rest of the butter, ¼ cup [25 g / 1 oz] flour and 1 cup [225 ml / 8 fl oz] milk. Stir in the parmesan.
5. Cook spaghetti in boiling salt water until 'al dente' then drain and add to the fish sauce mixing gently.
6. Sprinkle bread crumbs over base of serving dish, spoon a layer of spaghetti sauce over base, top with some béchamel. Continue layering in this way finishing with béchamel.
7. Bake in the oven for 15 minutes until golden. Serve at once.

Spaghetti al dolce

Sweet-Style Spaghetti

| | 00:15 | | 00:10 | |

American	Ingredients	Metric/Imperial
14 oz	Thin spaghetti (fidelini)	400 g / 14 oz
Scant ¼ cup	Vegetable oil	3 tbsp
2 tbsp	Vinegar	1 ½ tbsp
	Salt and pepper	
1	Red beetroot, cooked	1
3	Medium-sized carrots	3
2	White celery stalks	2
1 cup	Mayonnaise	225 ml / 8 fl oz

1. Cook spaghetti in boiling salted water until 'al dente'. Beat the oil, vinegar, salt and pepper together. Drain pasta and toss in some of the dressing.
2. Peel beetroot, dice into small cubes and put in a bowl.

Scrape carrots, grate finely and add to the beetroot; slice celery thinly and add to bowl. Toss vegetables in prepared dressing and mayonnaise and stir into spaghetti. Mix carefully and serve cold.

Variation: canned white tuna fish may be added with the vegetables.

Pasticcio di fegatini e maccheroni

Chicken Livers and Macaroni Pie

00:30   00:40

American	Ingredients	Metric/Imperial
1	Onion	1
1	Celery	1
2	Leeks	2
2	Carrots	2
⅓ cup	Butter	65 g / 2½ oz
	Salt and pepper	
1¼ cups	Tomato sauce (see page 79)	300 ml / ½ pint
8	Chicken livers	8
2 cups	Béchamel sauce	450 ml / ¾ pint
1 lb	Macaroni	450 g / 1 lb
¼ cup	Grated parmesan cheese	25 g / 1 oz

1. Preheat oven to 375°F / 190°C / Gas Mark 5. Grease an overproof serving dish.
2. Peel and chop onion, slice celery, leeks and carrots. Heat most of the butter and, when foaming, sauté the vegetables for 5 minutes, season and stir in tomato sauce.
3. Chop trimmed chicken livers into small pieces and add to the pan. Cook for 5 minutes stirring from time to time. Remove pan from heat.
4. Make a béchamel sauce. Cook macaroni in boiling salted water until 'al dente', drain and spoon half over the base of dish. Top with half the liver and vegetable mixture. Continue layering pasta and liver sauce, then cover with béchamel.
5. Sprinkle with parmesan, dot with dabs of remaining butter and bake for 30 minutes until golden brown. Serve hot.

Pasta con coniglio alla sarda

Sardinian-Style Rabbit with Pasta

	00:25		00:30
American	**Ingredients**	**Metric/Imperial**	
¾ lb	Rabbit meat, raw or cooked	350 g / 12 oz	
2 tbsp	Oil	1 ½ tbsp	
1	Sprig of sage	1	
1	Sprig of myrtle	1	
½ cup	White wine	125 ml / 4 fl oz	
½ cup	Stock	125 ml / 4 fl oz	
	Salt and pepper		
14 oz	Pasta	400 g / 14 oz	
1 cup	Coffee (single) cream	225 ml / 8 fl oz	

1. Grind (mince) rabbit meat finely. Heat oil and quickly brown meat with sage and myrtle. Pour over wine and stock, season, cover and simmer for 20 minutes.
2. Meanwhile cook pasta in boiling salted water until 'al dente', then drain.
3. Purée rabbit sauce in a blender or food processor, stir in cream, add drained pasta, and mix well. Serve immediately.

Penne e beccacce

Penne Pasta and Woodcocks

	00:20		00:50
American	**Ingredients**	**Metric/Imperial**	
2	Oven-ready woodcocks	2	
1	Onion	1	
¼ cup	Vegetable oil	50 ml / 2 fl oz	
½ cup	Butter	100 g / 4 oz	
¼ tsp	Sage	¼ tsp	
¼ tsp	Thyme	¼ tsp	
¼ tsp	Sweet marjoram	¼ tsp	
¼ tsp	Rosemary	¼ tsp	
¼ tsp	Chervil	¼ tsp	
2	Garlic cloves	2	
	Salt and pepper		
¼ cup	Cognac	50 ml / 2 fl oz	
½ lb	Strained tomato pulp	225 g / 8 oz	
14 oz	Penne pasta	400 g / 14 oz	
6 oz	Fresh fontina cheese	175 g / 6 oz	
	Truffle		

1. Cut all flesh from woodcocks into small pieces. Peel and chop onion.
2. Heat oil and butter together and, when foaming, brown

meat, stirring all the time. Add onion, herbs, garlic, salt, pepper and cognac to the pan with the tomato pulp. Cook for a further 45 minutes until woodcock is done.
3. Cook pasta in boiling salted water until 'al dente', then drain. Cut fontina into thin slices and mix into the pasta with the woodcock sauce.
4. Serve on a hot serving dish garnished with grated truffle.

Pizzoccheri ai colombacci

Pizzoccheri with Wood Pigeons

	00:15		00:50	

American	Ingredients	Metric/Imperial
2	Oven-ready wood pigeons	2
1	Onion	1
¼ cup	Lard	50 g / 2 oz
½ cup	Red wine	125 ml / 4 fl oz
2 or 3	Sage leaves	2 or 3
1 cup	Coffee (single) cream	225 ml / 8 fl oz
14 oz	Pizzoccheri	400 g / 14 oz
10 oz	Bitto cheese	275 g / 10 oz

1. Remove all flesh from the bones of the pigeons, and cut into even-sized pieces. Peel and chop onion, heat lard and when hot brown pigeon flesh lightly, stirring from time to time.
2. Pour the red wine into the pan, add onion and sage leaves, cover and simmer a further 45 minutes. Cool slightly, then stir in cream and keep warm over a low heat.
3. Cook pizzoccheri in boiling unsalted water until 'al dente'. Drain, stir in the bitto cheese, and cream sauce. Serve immediately.

Pennette alla contadina

Peasant Quills

	00:10		00:20	

American	Ingredients	Metric/Imperial
8	Tomatoes	8
3 tbsp	Olive oil	2 tbsp
1	Garlic clove	1
1 tbsp	Oregano	1 tbsp
	Salt and pepper	
14 oz	Pennette pasta	400 g / 14 oz
	Grated cheese as required	

1. Skin tomatoes and quarter. Heat oil in a pan and when hot fry crushed garlic, tomatoes and oregano for 5 minutes. Season and simmer for 10 minutes.
2. Cook pennette in boiling salted water until 'al dente', drain and stir into tomato sauce.
3. Spoon onto a serving dish, sprinkle with black pepper and grated cheese. Serve very hot.

Pasta del pirata Barbanera

Pirate Barbanera's Pasta

	00:10	01:15

American	Ingredients	Metric/Imperial
1	Onion	1
4	Garlic cloves	4
3 tbsp	Olive oil	2 tbsp
¼ tsp	Rosemary	¼ tsp
1	Chilli pepper	1
¾ lb	Ripe plum tomatoes	350 g / 12 oz
	White wine as required	
14 oz	Spaghetti or trenette (long narrow noodles)	400 g / 14 oz
4	Garlic cloves (optional)	4

1. Peel and finely chop onion and garlic. Heat oil in a pan and when hot add onion, garlic, rosemary and deseeded, chopped chilli and cook for 3 minutes.
2. Purée tomatoes and add to pan. Cover and simmer over a very low heat for 1 hour, adding white wine if sauce becomes too thick.
3. Cook spaghetti or trenette in boiling salted water until 'al dente', drain and put in a serving bowl. If liked add a further 4 cloves of crushed garlic to sauce, pour tomato sauce over pasta, stir well and serve.

Sformato di maccheroncelli

Small Macaroni Mold

	00:20	01:00

American	Ingredients	Metric/Imperial
1	Bread roll	1
	Milk as required	
1¾ cups	Ground (minced) meat	400g / 14 oz
2	Eggs	2
3 tbsp	Grated cheese	2 tbsp
	White flour, as required	
½ cup	Vegetable oil	125 ml / 4 fl oz
1	Large onion	1
6 - 7	Plum tomatoes (fresh or canned)	6 - 7
2	Garlic cloves	2
½ tsp	Oregano	½ tsp
½ tsp	Basil	½ tsp
	Salt and pepper	
¾ lb	Small macaroni	350 g / 12 oz
1	Scamorza cheese	1

1. Preheat oven to 375°F / 190°C / Gas Mark 5.
2. Soak inside of roll in milk, then squeeze out excess liquid. Mix ground meat with beaten eggs, the soaked bread crumbs

and grated cheese. Mix all ingredients well, divide mixture into even-sized small balls and toss in flour.

3. Heat all but 2 tablespoons of the oil in a frying pan and, when very hot, fry meat balls until evenly browned — about 5-8 minutes, then drain on absorbent paper.

4. Peel and slice onion, sieve tomatoes. Heat remaining oil in another pan and cook onion and crushed garlic for 5 minutes until golden brown. Add tomatoes, oregano, basil and pepper, then the meat balls. Cover and simmer for about 20 minutes.

5. Meanwhile cook small macaroni until 'al dente' in boiling salted water, drain then add meat balls and sauce. Skin and dice scamorza cheese and stir into pasta mixture.

6. Spoon pasta and sauce into an ovenproof serving dish. Bake for 25 minutes until a golden brown crust forms. Serve with grated cheese.

Bucatini al garganello

Bucatini with Teal

	00:35		00:60

American	Ingredients	Metric/Imperial
1	Small teal (wild duck)	1
2	Lemons	2
4	Anchovies	4
1 oz	Capers	25 g / 1 oz
½ cup	Butter	100 g / 4 oz
3 tbsp	Flour	2 tbsp
½ cup	Concentrated clear soup	125 ml / 4 fl oz
½ cup	Strong red wine	125 ml / 4 fl oz
	Salt and pepper	
¼ tsp	Nutmeg	¼ tsp
14 oz	Bucatini pasta	400 g / 14 oz

1. Clean the teal with water and rub over with a slice of lemon, then cut into pieces.

2. Chop anchovies and capers, sprinkle with lemon juice.

3. Melt 2 tablespoons [25 g / 1 oz] butter in a saucepan, add the white flour, mix well and add the mixture of soup and red wine. Add the chopped anchovies and capers, mix well and then add pieces of teal. Cook over a moderate heat until tender.

4. Remove the teal and take off all the flesh. Chop finely or blend the meat in an electric food blender or processor, add the sauce, season, mix well and warm again.

5. Cook the bucatini pasta in boiling salted water, drain when 'al dente' and dress the pasta with the teal sauce.

Rigatoni con le zucchine

Rigatoni with Gourds

	00:10		00:40

American	Ingredients	Metric/Imperial
14 oz	Gourds	400 g / 14 oz
Scant ¼ cup	Vegetable oil	3 tbsp
1	Garlic clove	1
	Salt and pepper	
1 tbsp	Chopped parsley	1 tbsp
14 oz	Rigatoni	400 g / 14 oz
¼ cup	Grated parmesan cheese	25 g / 1 oz

1. Wash gourds and slice thinly.

2. Heat oil and, when hot, add crushed garlic and cook for 1 minute. Put prepared gourds in pan, season, add chopped parsley, cover and cook for 40 minutes over a low heat, stirring from time to time.

3. Cook rigatoni in plenty of boiling salted water until 'al dente', drain and put in a serving bowl. Stir in the cooked gourds and sprinkle over parmesan cheese, just before serving.

Tagliatelle alle cipolle e porro

Noodles with Onions and Leek

	00:05		00:15

American	Ingredients	Metric/Imperial
2	Onions	2
1	Leek	1
1	Bunch of chives	1
1	Bunch of parsley	1
½ cup	Vegetable oil	125 ml / 4 fl oz
14 oz	Noodles	400 g / 14 oz
	Salt	
1 tbsp	Grated pecorino cheese	1 tbsp

1. Finely chop onions and leek with chives and parsley. Heat oil and cook half the vegetable and herb mixture for 3-5 minutes, stirring all the time.

2. Cook the noodles in the boiling salted water until 'al dente', drain and stir in the grated pecorino cheese and the hot vegetable mixture.

3. Finally stir in remaining raw chopped vegetables.

4. Spoon onto a hot serving dish and serve immediately.

Tagliatelle alla russa

Russian-Style Noodles

00:05   00:10

American	Ingredients	Metric/Imperial
1 tbsp	Butter	1 tbsp
1 cup	Coffee (single) cream	225 ml / 8 fl oz
	Salt and pepper	
7 oz can	Russian crab	200 g / 7 oz can
1 tsp	Vodka	1 tsp
½ lb	Noodles	225 g / 8 oz

1. Melt butter in a pan, add cream, salt, pepper, flaked crab and vodka. Simmer gently for 5 minutes. Do not allow to boil.
2. Cook noodles in boiling salted water until 'al dente', drain and stir into crab sauce. Spoon onto a hot serving dish and serve immediately.

Bavette e pesce

Noodles and Fish

This delicious pasta dish is eaten throughout Versilia, but even more in the south. It is essential to use fresh fish or left-over boiled fish, sieved carefully. A typical seaside dish which has several names and is often enjoyed near the Mediterranean.

00:40   00:60

American	Ingredients	Metric/Imperial
1 ½ lb	Fish	600 g / 1 ½ lb
1	Piece of skate	1
1	Piece of octopus	1
¼ cup	Oil	3 tbsp
2	Onions	2
1	Red chilli pepper	1
1 tbsp	Parsley	1 tbsp
¼ tsp	Basil	¼ tsp
2	Garlic cloves	2
1 cup	Strained tomato pulp	225 ml / 8 fl oz
1	Sweet yellow pepper	1
⅔ cup	Shelled, cooked prawns	100 g / 4 oz
	Salt and pepper	
14 oz	Noodles	400 g / 14 oz

1. Boil the fish in salted water, drain when firm, cool and remove the bones.
2. Pass the fish flesh through the blender, then tip it into a large saucepan with oil and peeled chopped onions.
3. Add chopped chilli pepper already deseeded, some chopped parsley and basil and 2 crushed cloves of garlic. Cook for about 10 minutes, mixing thoroughly, add the strained tomato pulp and a sweet yellow pepper cut into thin strips. Continue to cook the sauce, stirring from time to time. Add prawns and season well.
4. Cook the noodles in plenty of salted water. Drain them well while still firm and add to the sauce, stir for a few moments, increasing the heat, then serve, if possible in the cooking pot.

Tagiatelle alle cozze

Noodles with Mussels

American	Ingredients	Metric/Imperial
2 lb	Mussels	1 kg /2 lb
2	Garlic cloves	2
1 tbsp	Chopped parsley	1 tbsp
Scant ¼ cup	Vegetable oil	3 tbsp
½ cup	Whipping (double) cream	100 ml / 3½ fl oz
	Salt and pepper	
14 oz	Noodles	400 g / 14 oz
¼ cup	Butter	50 g / 2 oz
2	Egg yolks	2

1. Preheat oven to 325°F / 160°C / Gas Mark 3. Butter a large piece of foil and place on a heatproof serving dish.
2. Wash and scrub mussels individually in three changes of water and remove beards. Put in a large pan of water, bring to the boil and cook for 8-10 minutes until all the mussel shells have opened. Discard any closed mussel shells. Remove the moluscs carefully from the shells and leave on one side. Retain the cooking liquid.
3. Finely chop garlic and parsley. Heat oil in a pan and when very hot add garlic and parsley and cook for 1 minute then add mussels, seasoning and half the cooking water used for the mussels. Boil until liquid has reduced by half, then stir in cream and simmer for 3 minutes.
4. Cook noodles in boiling salted water until 'al dente', drain and put in a serving bowl. Add mussel sauce and butter and stir in well with the beaten egg yolks.
5. Spoon noodle mixture over foil in dish, close up foil to form a parcel. Bake for 10 minutes and serve 'parcel' in the dish at the table.

Pizzoccheri valtellinesi

Valtellina Noodles

American	Ingredients	Metric/Imperial
¾ lb	Mixed valtellina cheeses	350 g / 12 oz
3	Potatoes	3
¾ lb	Green vegetables (spinach, beet, savoy cabbage)	350 g / 12 oz
2	Garlic cloves	2
1	Large onion	1
14 oz	Pizzoccheri	400 g / 14 oz
1 tbsp	Butter	1 tbsp

1. Cut valtellina cheeses — a mixture of bitto, magnuca and toma — into small cubes. Dice peeled potatoes, trim green vegetables and shred. Chop garlic and onion.
2. Make pasta according to recipe for pizzoccheri pasta. Boil potatoes and vegetables separately in salted water.
3. In a small pan heat butter and fry chopped garlic and onion for 3 minutes. When vegetables are almost cooked, add pizzoccheri to saucepan. When pasta is 'al dente', drain with

the vegetables. Stir in garlic and onion mixture, then mix in the pieces of cheese.

4. Spoon into an ovenproof serving dish and place under a hot broiler [grill] to brown. Serve at once.

Tagliatelle alla veneta

Venetian-Style Noodles

	00:40	00:40

American	Ingredients	Metric/Imperial
14 oz	Mixed veal meat skinned and chopped	400 g / 14 oz
5 oz	Sausage	150 g / 5 oz
1	Onion	1
¼ cup	Butter.	50 g / 2 oz
	Salt and pepper	
¼ tsp	Nutmeg	¼ tsp
½ cup	Strong red wine	125 ml / 4 fl oz
1 cup	Cream	225 ml / 8 fl oz
14 oz	Noodles	400 g / 14 oz
	Plenty of grated parmesan cheese	

1. Chop veal and sausage into small pieces. Peel and chop onion. Heat butter in a pan and when foaming fry veal and sausage for 5 minutes, stirring all the time, until lightly browned. Add salt, pepper, nutmeg and wine to pan with onion and cream. Leave to simmer for about 30 minutes over a very low heat.

2. Cook pasta in boiling salted water until 'al dente', drain, stir in grated parmesan and hot meat sauce. Serve immediately.

Tagliatelle al caviale e panna

Noodles with Caviar and Cream

	00:05	00:15

American	Ingredients	Metric/Imperial
1 cup	Coffee (single) cream	225 ml / 8 fl oz
1	Small jar of caviar or substitute	1
1 tbsp	Butter	1 tbsp
2 or 3	Sage leaves	2 or 3
¼ cup	Cognac (optional)	50 ml / 2 fl oz
14 oz	Egg noodles	400 g / 14 oz
3 tbsp	Grated parmesan cheese	2 tbsp

1. Pour cream into a saucepan, add caviar and simmer over a low heat for 10 minutes, stirring all the time, but do not allow to boil. Add butter, sage and cognac and cook for a further 2 minutes.

2. Cook noodles in plenty of boiling salted water until 'al dente', drain and stir into caviar sauce with grated parmesan.

3. Spoon onto a hot serving dish and serve immediately.

Tagliatelle al capriolo

Roebuck Noodles

	00:20		00:40

American	Ingredients	Metric/Imperial
14 oz	Roebuck (venison) meat	400 g / 14 oz
1 cup	Whipping (double) cream	225 ml / 8 fl oz
1 cup	Milk	225 ml / 8 fl oz
½ cup	Cognac	125 ml / 4 fl oz
1	Onion	1
1	Bunch of chervil	1
	Salt and pepper	
14 oz	Fresh noodles	400 g / 14 oz
	Black truffle (optional)	

1. Cut roebuck meat into small pieces and put in a pan with cream, milk and three quarters of the cognac. Peel and chop onion, chop chervil and add to pan and cook over a very low heat for 40 minutes, stirring from time to time. Season with salt and pepper.
2. When meat is cooked, add remaining cognac, keep sauce warm over a very low heat.
3. Meanwhile cook tagliatelle in boiling salted water until 'al dente', drain and stir in prepared sauce.
4. Spoon onto a hot serving dish and garnish with a sprinkling of truffle if wished.

Tagliatelle verdi gratinate

Gratinated Green Noodles

	00:10		00:45

American	Ingredients	Metric/Imperial
¾ lb	Noodles	350 g / 12 oz
1 cup	Béchamel sauce	225 ml / 8 fl oz
5 oz	Mushrooms	150 g / 5 oz
½ lb	Ham cut into dice	225 g / 8 oz
	Butter as required	
1 tbsp	Bread crumbs	1 tbsp
2	Eggs	2
	Salt and pepper	
1 tbsp	Grated parmesan cheese	1 tbsp
1 cup	Cream	225 ml / 8 fl oz
2 tsp	Curry powder	2 tsp
	Black or powdered truffle (optional)	

1. Heat oven to 350°F / 180°C / Gas Mark 4.
2. Parboil noodles for 5 minutes, then drain and rinse under cold water. Prepare a cup of béchamel.
3. Add mushrooms and ham to the béchamel, blend with the noodles, mixing carefully.

4. Butter an ovenproof dish, scatter with bread crumbs and slip mixture into it. Beat eggs with salt, pepper and parmesan and pour over the noodle mixture.

5. Place dish in centre of the oven and bake for 20-25 minutes until a golden crust forms.

6. Meanwhile beat cream with the curry powder. Add grated black truffle (or powdered form) to sauce. Pour into a sauceboat and serve cold as an accompaniment to the dish of hot gratinated noodles.

Bavette alla livornese

Leghorn-Style Noodles

00:25   00:35

American	Ingredients	Metric/Imperial
3 tbsp	Oil	2 tbsp
4	Red rock mullet	4
1	Onion	1
1	Garlic clove	1
½ lb	Peeled tomatoes	225 g / 8 oz
	Salt and pepper	
1 ½ tsp	Chopped basil	1 ½ tsp
14 oz	Noodles, fresh or dried	400 g / 14 oz

1. Heat the oil in a frying pan, add the well-cleaned mullet, a chopped onion, crushed garlic, peeled tomatoes, salt, pepper, and 1 teaspoon of basil and cook gently; turn the fish over only once. (The fish will be cooked when the eyes appear white.)

2. Remove the fish without breaking, open and bone carefully.

3. Beat the fish flesh with the cooking liquid, then return to a small saucepan to thicken well.

4. Heat plenty of salted water in a large saucepan, add the noodles when the water is boiling and cook until firm. Drain and season at once with the mullet sauce. Sprinkle with basil.

Tagliatelle al mascarpone

Mascarpone Noodles

	00:15		00:10

American	Ingredients	Metric/Imperial
7 oz	Mascarpone cheese	200 g / 7 oz
2	Egg yolks	2
½ cup	Grated parmesan cheese	50g / 2 oz
14 oz	Noodles	400 g / 14 oz
	Salt and pepper	

1. Put mascarpone in a bowl and beat with a wooden spoon. Add egg yolks and grated parmesan. Continue to mix until ingredients are well blended to a soft cream consistency.
2. Boil noodles in boiling salted water until 'al dente'. Drain and stir in the mascarpone cream. Sprinkle with freshly-ground pepper and serve piping hot.

Fettuccine dorate

Golden Noodles

	00:10		00:20

American	Ingredients	Metric/Imperial
	Salt	
14 oz	Noodles	400 g / 14 oz
4 tbsp	Margarine	50 g / 2 oz
3 tbsp	Bread crumbs	2 tbsp
1 tsp	Chopped basil	1 tsp
	Pepper	
	Pecorino cheese as desired	

1. Bring to the boil a large saucepan of salted water, drop in the egg noodles, drain when cooked 'al dente'.
2. Heat the margarine in a frying pan, lightly brown the bread crumbs and the very finely chopped basil in the fat, add the drained noodles and cook till golden over a brisk heat. Season and sprinkle with grated strong pecorino.

Agnolotti alla parmense

Parmesan Ravioli

	00:60	00:12 to 00:18
		depending on size

American	Ingredients	Metric/Imperial
½ cup	Grated stale bread	50 g / 2 oz
1 cup	Grated parmesan cheese	100 g / 4 oz
	Salt and pepper	
½ tsp	Nutmeg	½ tsp
1 lb	Pasta dough	450 g / 1 lb

1. Mix the bread, grated parmesan, salt and pepper with the nutmeg, blending together well.
2. Prepare the pasta by halving the dough, rolling 2 pieces out thinly on the table.
3. Place little heaps of filling on one half, cover with the remaining half of the dough and shape some perfectly round agnolotti with a small glass or cutter.
4. Heat plenty of salted water in a saucepan and when the water comes to the boil, toss in ravioli and serve them with meat sauce or in clear soup.
5. Serve grated parmesan separately with this delicately flavored dish.

Ravioli alla Val Passiria

Passer Valley Ravioli

	01:00	00:15

American	Ingredients	Metric/Imperial
1 lb	Pasta dough	450 g / 1 lb
2	Potatoes	2
2	Eggs	2
1	Bunch of mint	1
¼ lb	Ricotta cheese	100 g / 4 oz
	Salt and pepper	
¼ tsp	Nutmeg	¼ tsp
1 tsp	Bread crumbs	1 tsp
1 ¼ lb	Tender green beans	600 g / 1 ¼ lb
1 tbsp	Butter	1 tbsp
1 tbsp	Grated parmesan cheese	1 tbsp

1. Prepare pasta dough using basic recipe.
2. Peel the potatoes and boil until tender, drain and mash. Add 2 beaten eggs, mint, ricotta, salt, pepper, nutmeg and bread crumbs and mix to form a firm mixture.
3. Prepare ravioli using potato and ricotta filling following procedure opposite for 'Port Maurice little ravioli'.
4. Put on a large wide pan of salted water and bring to the boil, then cook beans until just tender, drain and keep warm. Drop in ravioli, simmer for 6-8 minutes until tender when ravioli will rise to surface.
5. Remove carefully using a slotted spoon and put on a hot serving dish. Mix in beans, dot with butter, sprinkle with parmesan and serve immediately.

Preparing Small Ravioli
Mix the meat filling, egg and grated parmesan cheese in a bowl, moistening with white wine if necessary. Cool

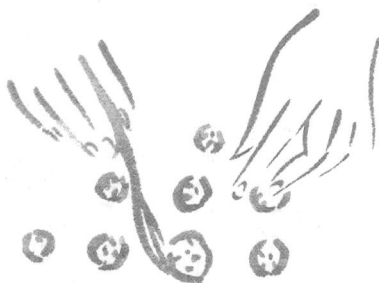

Place teaspoonfuls of the prepared filling on one half of the rolled out dough

Fold the rest of the dough over and press down between the rows of filling. Cut out with the ravioli cutter

Cook the pasta in a saucepan of boiling salted water. Then serve tossed in butter and sprinkled with grated parmesan

Ravioli alle noci

Ravioli with Walnuts

00:20   00:10

American	Ingredients	Metric/Imperial
½	Bread roll	½
	Milk	
20	Shelled walnuts	20
½	Garlic clove	½
Scant ¼ cup	Vegetable oil	3 tbsp
¼ cup	Grated cheese	25 g / 1 oz
¼ tsp	Marjoram	¼ tsp
	Salt and pepper	
¼ cup	Coffee (single) cream	50 ml / 2 fl oz
1 ¼ lb	Ravioli (without meat)	600 g / 1 ¼ lb
1 tbsp	Butter	1 tbsp

1. Soak bread crumbs from roll in milk, then squeeze and put in blender with walnuts, garlic, oil, cheese, marjoram, salt, pepper and cream. Blend until a thick purée is formed, then put in a pan over a low heat to heat through whilst ravioli cooks.
2. Cook ravioli in boiling salted water for 6 - 8 minutes then carefully remove with a slotted spoon and place on a hot serving dish.
3. Pour walnut sauce over pasta, add a few dabs of butter and serve immediately.

Raviolini al gratin

Little Ravioli au Gratin

00:15   01:00

American	Ingredients	Metric/Imperial
1	Small onion	1
3 tbsp	Butter	2 tbsp
5 oz	Ham cooked in a single slice	150 g / 5 oz
1 cup	Frozen peas	150 g / 5 oz
	Salt and pepper	
3	Peeled tomatoes	3
14 oz	Ravioli	400 g / 14 oz
¼ lb	Sliced fontina	100 g / 4 oz
1 tbsp	Grated cheese	1 tbsp

1. Preheat oven to 400°F / 200°C / Gas Mark 6. Grease an ovenproof dish.
2. Peel and slice onion. Melt half the butter and fry the onion for 2 - 3 minutes. Dice ham, add to pan and cook a further minute, then add the peas, salt, pepper and crushed tomatoes. Cook for 10 minutes.
3. Meanwhile cook the ravioli in the boiling salted water for 6-8 minutes. Remove with a slotted spoon. Put half ravioli over the base of the dish, top with slices of fontina cheese and pour over half the tomato sauce. Continue layering in this way with ravioli and sauce, then sprinkle top with grated cheese and add dabs of butter.
4. Bake for 30 minutes until golden and crusty. Serve hot.

Ravioli alla mantovana

Mantuan-Style Ravioli

	00:40	00:20

American	Ingredients	Metric/Imperial
¾ lb	Mixed herbs	350 g / 12 oz
1 cup	Grated parmesan cheese	100 g / 4 oz
¾ lb	Ricotta cheese	350 g / 12 oz
1	Egg	1
	Salt and pepper	
	Meat sauce (see page 74)	
	Grated parmesan cheese	
14 oz	Pasta dough	400 g / 14 oz

1. Wash and boil herbs in salted water for 5 minutes, drain and squeeze out well, then chop finely. Mix herbs with parmesan, ricotta and egg to obtain a smooth mixture. Season with salt and pepper.
2. Roll out the dough very finely and make ricotta filled ravioli, following procedure for 'Port Maurice little ravioli'.
3. Prepare a large wide pan with a plenty of boiling salted water and drop in ravioli. Simmer until tender for 6-8 minutes when ravioli will rise to surface.
4. Remove carefully with a slotted spoon and place on a hot serving dish. Serve with a meat sauce and parmesan.

Raviolini alla Porto Maurizio

Port Maurice Little Ravioli

	00:30	00:45

American	Ingredients	Metric/Imperial
Scant ¼ cup	Vegetable oil	3 tbsp
1 ½ cups	Ground (minced) meat or left-over roast or boiled meat	350 g / 12 oz
½ tsp	Sage	½ tsp
½ tsp	Rosemary	½ tsp
½ tsp	Thyme	½ tsp
½ tsp	Sweet marjoram	½ tsp
½ tsp	Basil	½ tsp
2	Bay leaves	2
	Salt and pepper	
1	Egg	1
1 tbsp	Grated cheese	1 tbsp
¼ tsp	Nutmeg	¼ tsp
For the pasta		
3 ½ cups	White flour	400 g / 14 oz
4	Eggs	4
1 tsp	Fine salt	1 tsp

1. Heat oil until very hot, fry meat until lightly browned all over. Add sage, rosemary, thyme, sweet marjoram, basil, bay, salt and pepper. Allow to simmer for 30 minutes stirring from time to time, then remove from heat and leave to cool.

2. Grind meat and herb mixture in a food processor until very fine. Add beaten egg, cheese, nutmeg and seasoning to forcemeat and mix thoroughly to obtain a smooth mixture.

3. Prepare pasta according to basic recipe.

4. Roll out pasta on a floured board into 4 equal thin oblongs. On one sheet drop tiny mounds of filling 1½ in / 4 cm apart in straight lines. Brush water in straight lines between mounds. Place a sheet of dough evenly over the top. Working quickly press down between each mound of filling along wetted line to form 2 in / 5 cm squares. Cut pasta into squares using a pastry cutter or wheel. Separate squares and put on a floured tea towel. Repeat with remaining pasta and filling.

5. Prepare a large wide pan with plenty of boiling salted water and drop in ravioli. Simmer for 6-8 minutes, when ravioli will rise to surface. Remove with a slotted spoon and place on a hot serving dish.

6. Serve with a tomato sauce poured over ravioli.

Agnolotti

Small Ravioli

	00:30	00:08 to 00:10	
	The pasta dough 01:00		

American	Ingredients	Metric/Imperial
¼ cup	Butter	50 g / 2 oz
¼ lb	Veal	100 g / 4 oz
5 oz	Lean pork	150 g / 5 oz
	Salt and pepper	
5 oz	Chopped raw ham	150 g / 5 oz
1	Truffle (optional)	1
1	Egg, beaten	1
¼ cup	Grated parmesan cheese	25 g / 1 oz
	A little dry white wine (if required)	
	A sheet of fresh pasta dough	
	Grated parmesan cheese	
2 tbsp	Butter for seasoning	25 g / 1 oz

1. Melt butter in a saucepan, add the ground (minced) veal, pork, salt, pepper, chopped ham, half the truffle cut in fine slices, cook over a low heat.

2. Add the beaten egg and the grated cheese, mix all the ingredients thoroughly, cooking and moistening only if necessary with a little dry white wine. Allow to cool.

3. Make the pasta according to the basic recipe for fresh pasta. Roll out the dough in two equal pieces, on one half place spoonfuls of the prepared filling in little heaps. Fold the other half over, and then cut with the ravioli cutter to give the desired shape.

4. Continue with remaining dough and mixture. Leave the filled ravioli for 30 minutes.

5. Boil plenty of salted water in a large saucepan and as soon as it reaches boiling point, toss the pasta in.

6. The ravioli will be ready when they rise to the surface. Take out of the water with a slotted spoon, arrange on a hot serving dish. Toss in butter and sprinkle with grated parmesan cheese. Finally, scatter with fine slices of the remaining truffle and serve.

Ravioli verdi alla ricotta

Green Ravioli with Ricotta

| | 01:15 | 00:12 | |

American	Ingredients	Metric/Imperial
3½ cups	Flour	400 g / 14 oz
4	Eggs	4
	Salt	
7	Sprigs of parsley	7
2 or 3	Basil leaves	2 or 3
¾ lb	Ricotta cheese	350 g / 12 oz
½ cup	Grated parmesan cheese	50 g / 2 oz
¼ tsp	Nutmeg	¼ tsp
	Butter and nutmeg for seasoning	

1. Prepare pasta dough according to basic recipe using flour, eggs, a few drops green colouring and salt (see page 94) and leave to stand, wrapped in foil.

2. Finely chop parsley, basil and ricotta and put in a bowl with remaining egg, parmesan, salt and nutmeg. Stir to mix well, then beat to a smooth mixture.

3. Roll out pasta dough into 4 equal thin oblongs. On one sheet drop tiny mounds of filling 1½ in / 4 cm apart. Brush water between mounds and place a sheet of dough evenly over the top. Press dough firmly down between mounds of filling to form 2 in / 5 cm squares. Cut into squares using pastry wheel or cutter. Repeat with remaining dough and filling.

4. Bring a pan of salted water to the boil and drop in ravioli. Boil 5-6 minutes. Remove carefully with a slotted spoon, place on a hot serving dish and dot with butter and nutmeg.

Gnocchi fritti senza ripieno

Fried Gnocchi without Filling

	00:20		00:05	

American	Ingredients	Metric/Imperial
2 cups	White flour or finely ground semolina	225 g / 8 oz
½ tsp	Salt	½ tsp
2 tbsp	Lard	25 g / 1 oz
	Oil for deep frying	

1. Knead flour with a little water, salt, and the lard and roll out paste to a very thin layer. Cut into squares and prick with a fork.

2. Heat oil in a large heavy based pan, fitted with a basket and fry squares for 2 minutes, then drain on absorbent paper.

3. Fried gnocchi can be served as an hors d'oeuvre with cold dishes such as cooked pressed pork, mortadella, ham or various kinds of sausages.

Gnocchi alla veronese

Veronese-Style Gnocchi

	01:20		01:10	

American	Ingredients	Metric/Imperial
2 oz	Dried mushrooms	50 g / 2 oz
5 oz	Brains	150 g / 5 oz
3 tbsp	Vinegar	2 tbsp
½ cup	Butter	100 g / 4 oz
1	Onion	1
¼ cup	Brandy	50 ml / 2 fl oz
	Salt and pepper	
½ cup	Stock	125 ml / 4 fl oz
1 lb	Gnocchi or pasta	450 g / 1 lb
2½ cups	Béchamel sauce	600 ml / 1 pint
¼ cup	Grated parmesan cheese	25 g / 1 oz
¼ cup	Bread crumbs	25 g / 1 oz

1. Preheat the oven to 400°F / 200°C / Gas Mark 6.

2. Steep the mushrooms in hot water for 1 hour, drain well.

3. Soak the brains in vinegar and water.

4. Heat the butter in a pan over a low heat, add the chopped onion and the mushrooms.

5. Drain the brains, pat dry with absorbent kitchen paper. Cut into small pieces, add to the mixture in the frying pan with the brandy, season with salt and pepper, mix in the stock and cook for about 45 minutes, pouring in additional stock if necessary.

6. Cook the gnocchi in a saucepan with plenty of salted water, drain them and place them in a buttered ovenproof dish. Cover with the béchamel sauce and sprinkle them with a generous amount of grated parmesan and bread crumbs. Place in the oven for about 20 minutes and serve immediately.

Gnocchi gialli

Yellow Gnocchi

🔪 00:60   00:20 🍲

American	Ingredients	Metric/Imperial
1¾ lb	Pumpkin pulp	800 g / 1¾ lb
¾ cup	Butter	175 g / 6 oz
	Salt and pepper	
¼ lb	Emmental cheese	100 g / 4 oz
¼ lb	Gouda cheese	100 g / 4 oz
¼ lb	Bergkase cheese	100 g / 4 oz
2	Eggs	2
1 cup	White flour	100 g / 4 oz
3	Sage leaves	3

1. Cut the pumpkin into small pieces. In a large saucepan melt about ½ cup [100 g / 4 oz] of butter, thin with a little water and add the pieces of pumpkin. Season with salt and sprinkle with freshly-ground pepper, allow to cook until, by stirring briskly, you succeed in obtaining a thick and smooth cream from the pumpkin. Remove from the heat and allow to stand.
2. Chop up all the cheeses and mix them together. Then add them to the pumpkin. Add the eggs and the flour and work until you obtain a fairly stiff mixture. Make many little gnocchi from the mixture.
3. Bring a large saucepan of salted water to the boil. Tip the gnocchetti in the water, in batches, for about 3 minutes and when they begin to float, take them out on a slotted spoon.
4. In a frying pan melt the rest of butter and flavour by adding sage leaves. Season the gnochetti with melted butter.

Gnocchetti alla Maddalena

Magdalene's Little Gnocchi

🔪 00:30   01:10 🍲

American	Ingredients	Metric/Imperial
3	Artichokes	3
1	Lemon	1
⅓ cup	Butter	75 g / 3 oz
½ cup	Oil	125 ml / 4 fl oz
	Salt and pepper	
2	Large chicken breasts	2
2	Garlic cloves	2
¼ tsp	Rosemary	¼ tsp
¼ tsp	Sage	¼ tsp
1	Stock cube	1
¾ lb	Little gnocchi made with hard-grain wheat or other pasta	350 g / 12 oz
¼ cup	Grated cheese	25 g / 1 oz

1. Preheat oven to 400°F / 200°C / Gas Mark 6.
2. Carefully clean the artichokes, removing the hardest leaves,

chokes and the spines, cut into thin slices and place them in water and lemon juice.

3. Melt half the butter in a large frying pan, add 3 tablespoons of oil and, when it begins to brown, add the well-drained artichokes, season with salt and pepper and cover with a lid. Cook on a very low heat, check from time to time and if the pan should become too dry, add a little hot water.

4. Clean the chicken breasts, cut them in small pieces. Heat the oil, garlic, rosemary and sage. When they are nicely browned, add salt and pepper and continue cooking, moistening with a little water and stock cube. Cook the chicken and the artichokes for about 45 minutes.

5. Heat a saucepan with plenty of salted water, bring it to the boil and cook the little gnocchi till 'al dente'. Drain the pasta well and season it with the artichokes and the chicken, mix and tip into an ovenproof dish. Sprinkle the surface with small dabs of the remaining butter and grated cheese. Place in the moderately hot oven and cook for about 15 minutes, until the surface is golden.

Gnocchi di patate

Potato Gnocchi with Cheese

	00:40	00:45	

American	Ingredients	Metric/Imperial
2 lb	Potatoes	1 kg / 2 lb
3 cups	All purpose (plain) flour	350 g / 12 oz
1	Egg	1
¼ lb	Mortadella sausage	100 g / 4 oz
¼ tsp	Nutmeg	¼ tsp
	Salt	
¼ lb	Mozzarella cheese	100 g / 4 oz
24	Sage leaves	24
1 tbsp	Butter	15 g / ½ oz
½ cup	Grated cheese	100 g / 4 oz

1. Preheat the oven to 400°F / 200°C / Gas Mark 6.

2. Boil the potatoes in cold salted water. When they are tender, drain and remove the skins and put through a ricer or food mill or coarse sieve.

3. Sprinkle some of the sifted flour on to the board, place the heap of potatoes in the centre and make a well in the centre. Add the egg, mixed with the finely chopped mortadella, nutmeg and salt, sprinkle in a little flour and mix together to be a fairly firm dough.

4. Roll the strips into thin sausage shapes and then cut off pieces 1½ in / 4 cm long. Mark on the rough side of a grater.

5. Cook in boiling salted water or stock for about 5 minutes until they start floating to the surface.

6. Arrange some slices of mozzarella on the bottom of a buttered ovenproof dish, sprinkle with grated cheese and arrange some leaves of sage on top.

7. Drain the gnocchi onto the cheese and sprinkle with the remaining cheese, bake in the oven for 20 minutes. Serve piping hot with a tomato sauce.

Potato Gnocchi
Sieve or grate the cooked potatoes

Add the egg, the sausage mixture and the flour and mix to form a moist dough

Cut and shape the gnocchi, using the back of a grater to mark the surface of the gnocchi with a regular pattern

Place the cooked gnocchi onto a layer of cheese and sage in an ovenproof dish

Gnocchetti di semola alle zucchine

Little Semolina Gnocchi with Gourds

| | 00:35 | | 00:30 | |

American	Ingredients	Metric/Imperial
4	Gourds	4
1 cup	Cream	225 ml / 8 fl oz
½ cup	Butter	100 g / 4 oz
¼ tsp	Nutmeg	¼ tsp
	Salt and pepper	
½ tsp	Cornstarch (cornflour)	½ tsp
14 oz	Pasta gnocchi	400 g / 14 oz
1 tbsp	Grated parmesan cheese	1 tbsp
1	Bunch of mint, chopped	1

1. Boil 2 gourds until they are 'al dente', then pass through the vegetable mill or blender.
2. Add the cream and put in a small saucepan with the butter (retaining a little for the pasta), nutmeg, salt and pepper. Gradually thicken this sauce, adding the cornstarch mixed with a few drops of water.
3. Boil the little gnocchi in salted water until 'al dente'. Drain and season them with cheese and a little butter.
4. Wash separately two raw tender gourds, and slice finely, if possible with a slicing machine. Slightly heat the sauce made with the sieved gourds and mix with the gnocchetti, complete with the slices of raw gourds, sprinkle with mint and serve.

Gnocchi filanti

Stringy Gnocchi

| | 00:15 | | 00:30 | |

American	Ingredients	Metric/Imperial
	Salt	
7 oz	Fontina cheese	200 g / 7 oz
1 cup	Coffee (single) cream	225 ml / 8 fl oz
½	Vegetable stock cube	½
	Pepper	
2 lb	Potato gnocchi	1 kg / 2 lb
4 tbsp	Grated parmesan cheese	3 tbsp

1. Bring to the boil a large saucepan of salted water.
2. Cut the fontina into small cubes. Heat the cream in a little pan and flavour it with half a stock cube and freshly-ground pepper. Add the fontina and remove it immediately after from the heat. Pour into a soup tureen.
3. Cook the gnocchi in the boiling water. When they begin to float to the surface, drain with a slotted spoon. Tip into the soup tureen, stir and serve sprinkled with plenty of grated parmesan.

Gnocchi verdi

Green Gnocchi

🔪 00:25		00:25 🥘
American	**Ingredients**	**Metric/Imperial**
1 lb	Spinach	500 g / 1 lb
	Salt and pepper	
14 oz	Very fresh ricotta cheese	400 g / 14 oz
2	Egg yolks	2
	All purpose (plain) flour	
2 tbsp	Butter	25 g / 1 oz
1 tbsp	Grated parmesan cheese	1 tbsp

1. Cook the spinach in boiling, salted water, for a few minutes.
2. Work the ricotta in an earthenware dish, mixing continuously with a wooden spoon.
3. Drain the spinach, chop and pass through a food processor or vegetable mill. Add the purée obtained to the ricotta and blend. Mix in the two egg yolks. Allow the mixture to stand for a few minutes then make it into many little gnocchi, with the aid of a spoon.
4. Flour a large pastry-board and, for convenience, lay the little gnocchi on it as you make them.
5. Heat a large saucepan of salted water, when it is boiling tip the gnocchi into it a few at a time. Leave them to cook for about 2 minutes. Drain them, without breaking.
6. Melt the butter and when it turns golden, remove from the heat and pour it over the gnocchi. Sprinkle with grated cheese, freshly-ground pepper, and serve.

Pizzicotti dei romani

Romans' Pinches

🔪 00:30		00:20 🥘
American	**Ingredients**	**Metric/Imperial**
1 ½ lb	Spinach	700 g / 1 ½ lb
	Salt and pepper	
¾ lb	Ricotta cheese	350 g / 12 oz
3	Eggs	3
Scant ¼ cup	Grated parmesan cheese	3 tbsp
¼ tsp	Nutmeg	¼ tsp
	Flour as required	
4 tbsp	Butter	50 g / 2 oz
Scant ¼ cup	Whipping (double) cream	3 tbsp
¼ tsp	Sage	¼ tsp
¼ tsp	Basil	¼ tsp
Scant ¼ cup	Grand Marnier	3 tbsp
3 tbsp	Grated cheese	2 tbsp

1. Clean spinach in several changes of water, put in a pan and cook for about 5 minutes over a medium heat. Season with salt and then press spinach well to remove all excess water.
2. Sieve spinach and ricotta cheese together into a bowl or blend in a food processor.
3. Add beaten eggs, parmesan cheese, salt, pepper and

nutmeg and blend all ingredients well together with the hands adding sufficient flour to form a smooth paste.

4. Grease hands and divide paste into small pieces the size of a cherry and roll each into a ball.

5. To make sauce, melt butter in a pan, add salt, pepper and cream and boil for 5 minutes. Stir in sage, basil and Grand Marnier, then the grated cheese.

6. Bring a pan of salted water to the boil and drop in balls of gnocci, poach until they rise and float on the water. Carefully remove with a slotted spoon.

7. Put the gnocchi in a serving bowl, top with the cream sauce and serve at once.

Lasagne verdi alla ligure

Ligurian-Style Green Lasagne

| | 00:40 | | 00:40 | |

American	Ingredients	Metric/Imperial
1 lb	Basic mixture for fresh pasta	500 g / 1 lb
1 lb	Nettles or beet	500 g / 1 lb
1	Egg	1
1 lb	Meat sauce (see page 74)	500 g / 1 lb
2½ cups	Béchamel	600 ml / 1 pint

1. Preheat oven to 350°F / 180°C / Gas Mark 4.

2. Make pasta.

3. Finely chop nettles or beet, boil in a little water then squeeze thoroughly to remove all water.

4. Blend the pressed vegetables with the pasta, adding a beaten egg. Roll out pasta dough thinly, cut out lasagne in desired shape.

5. Cook lasagne in boiling salted water, a few pieces at a time until 'al dente'. Lay pasta on a clean teatowel to dry thoroughly.

6. Grease an oblong ovenproof serving dish, place a layer of lasagne over base, top with a layer of meat sauce. Cover with more lasagne then sauce, ending with a layer of pasta.

7. Pour over béchamel and bake for 25 minutes. Serve hot.

Variation: lasagne can be cooked and served at once with garlic and basil sauce, fresh tomato or meat sauce, without baking.

Cannelloni alla siciliana

Sicilian-Style Cannelloni

⌦ 00:30   00:40 ⌫

American	Ingredients	Metric/Imperial
2 cups	Coffee (single) cream	450 ml / 16 fl oz
¾ lb	Ricotta cheese	350 g / 12 oz
2 oz	Softened pine nuts	50 g / 2 oz
⅓ cup	Raisins	50 g / 2 oz
1	Onion	1
	Salt and pepper	
½ tsp	Red paprika	½ tsp
½ lb	Cooked ham	225 g / 8 oz
½ cup	Dry marsala	125 ml / 4 fl oz
1 lb	Cannelloni	500 g / 1 lb
	Butter	
½ cup	Grated pecorino cheese	50 g / 2 oz
½ tsp	Cumin seeds	½ tsp

Preheat oven to 400°F / 200°C / Gas Mark 6.

1. Prepare the sauce by heating the cream over a low heat. Add the crumbled ricotta, pine nuts, raisins, finely chopped onion, salt, pepper, red paprika, the cooked ham, diced, and dry marsala. Allow the sauce to simmer over a very low heat.

2. Boil the cannelloni in salted water till firm to the bite, drain.

3. In a well-buttered ovenproof dish arrange a layer of cannelloni, cover with a little sauce, then sprinkle with grated pecorino. Continue with a layer of cannelloni, one of sauce and one of pecorino. Finish with a layer of sauce, sprinkle with plenty of pecorino and finally scatter with cumin seeds. Put in oven to cook for 25 minutes.

Cannelloni della nonna

Granny's Cannelloni

⌦ 00:40   00:40 ⌫

American	Ingredients	Metric/Imperial
¾ lb	Spinach	350 g / 12 oz
¾ lb	Braised meat	350 g / 12 oz
2	Eggs	2
7 tbsp	Grated cheese	5½ tbsp
	Salt and pepper	
¼ tsp	Nutmeg	¼ tsp
2½ cups	Béchamel	600 ml / 1 pint
12	Cannelloni or squares of fresh pasta	12
2 tbsp	Butter	25 g / 1 oz

1. Preheat the oven to 375°F / 190°C / Gas Mark 5.

2. Cook the spinach in very little salted water, drain and squeeze well, then pass through a vegetable mill, collecting the purée in an earthenware dish.

3. Chop the braised meat, removing any fat from it and add to the spinach, mix and blend with two egg yolks and most of the grated cheese. Season the filling with salt and pepper and a little grated nutmeg.

4. Cook the cannelloni in boiling salted water, drain on a table napkin or on absorbent kitchen paper.

5. Use a spoon to fill the cannelloni with the mixture of meat and spinach and arrange them in an ovenproof dish.

6. Prepare separately the béchamel sauce and pour over the cannelloni. Scatter with little dabs of butter, sprinkle with grated cheese and place in the oven for 30 minutes.

Lasagne piccanti

Spicy Lasagne

00:15   01:45

American	Ingredients	Metric/Imperial
1	Onion	1
1	Garlic clove	1
¼ lb	Sausage	100 g / 4 oz
1 oz	Dried mushrooms	25 g / 1 oz
Scant ¼ cup	Oil	3 tbsp
½ cup	Ground (minced) beef	100 g / 4 oz
1	Chilli pepper	1
½ cup	Red wine	125 ml / 4 fl oz
½ lb	Peeled tomatoes	225 g / 8 oz
	Salt and pepper	
6 tbsp	Flour	65 g / 1½ oz
3 tbsp	Butter	65 g / 1½ oz
2½ cups	Milk	600 ml / 1 pint
½ cup	Grated parmesan cheese	50 g / 2 oz
7 oz	Lasagne	200 g / 7 oz
7 oz	Noodles	200 g / 7 oz

1. Peel and chop onion, crush garlic clove, chop sausage and soften mushrooms in warm water for 10 minutes.

2. Heat half the oil in a pan, sauté the onions and the garlic for 2 minutes, add meat, sausage and drained mushrooms.
Cook a further 2-3 minutes. Add chopped deseeded chilli.

3. Pour in red wine, add tomatoes, season with salt and pepper and cook over a low heat for about 1 hour in an uncovered pan.

4. Preheat the oven to 350°F / 180°C / Gas Mark 4.

5. Meanwhile make béchamel sauce with the flour, butter and milk (see page 76). Finally stir in parmesan cheese.

6. Cook lasagne, a few sheets at a time, in boiling salted water with a dash of oil added until 'al dente'. Remove and rinse with cold water then dry on a tea towel.

7. Cook noodles in boiling salted water with a dash of oil added until 'al dente', drain and stir in the tomato sauce. Spoon mixture onto an oblong ovenproof serving dish.

8. Top with a layer of lasagne and finally pour over the béchamel sauce.

9. Bake in the oven for 30 minutes, then serve with a salad.

Lasagnette e lumache

Small Lasagne and Snails

🔪 00:10   00:45 🍲

American	Ingredients	Metric/Imperial
2 lb	Snails with the shell	1 kg / 2 lb
Scant ¼ cup	Oil	3 tbsp
1	Bunch of parsley	1
2	Garlic cloves	2
½ cup	White wine	125 ml / 4 fl oz
14 oz	Small lasagne	400 g / 14 oz
	Salt and pepper	

1. Preheat oven to 325°F / 170°C / Gas Mark 3.
2. Toss snails in boiling salted water for 10 minutes, drain and carefully remove snails from shells using a sharp-pronged fork.
3. Heat half of the oil in a pan, chop parsley and add to pan with crushed garlic. Cook for 1 minute, then add snails and cook a further 2-3 minutes to brown.
4. Pour in the wine and cook for 10 minutes. Cook lasagne in boiling salted water until 'al dente', drain, then add snail sauce to pasta with remaining oil.
5. Spoon into 4 individual ovenproof serving dishes, reheat in the oven for 15 minutes and serve.

Lasagne primavera

Springtime Lasagne

🔪 00:30   00:45 🍲

American	Ingredients	Metric/Imperial
3½ cups	Flour	400 g / 14 oz
4	Eggs	4
	Salt	
1 lb	Asparagus	500 g / 1 lb
½ tsp	Basil	½ tsp
1 cup	Coffee (single) cream	225 ml / 8 fl oz
2 tbsp	Butter	25 g / 1 oz
	Pepper	
1 cup	Béchamel	225 ml / 8 fl oz

1. Preheat the oven to 350°F / 180°C / Gas Mark 4.
2. Prepare pasta dough using flour, egg and salt (see page 94), and cut out lasagne, then cook in boiling salted water until 'al dente'. Rinse under cold water and dry. Put half the lasagne into a rectangular ovenproof serving dish.
3. Cook asparagus until just softened, then drain. Meanwhile add chopped basil, half the cream, half the butter, salt and pepper to the béchamel sauce. Stir in asparagus and spoon over lasagne in serving dish.
4. Top with remaining lasagne, pour over remaining cream and dab with butter.
5. Bake for 25-30 minutes and serve immediately.

SAUCES

SAUCES

Besciamella classica

Quick Béchamel Sauce

Apparently, this sauce, which is a delicious accompaniment to so many dishes, was invented by the Marquis of Béchamel who, unable to stand the complicated sauces of French cuisine, set about resolving his own gastronomical problems. But a sauce similar to béchamel was already well-known in Renaissance time and was served with every type of dish.

	00:05		00:15	

American	Ingredients	Metric/Imperial
¼ cup	Butter	50 g / 2 oz
½ cup	Flour or cornstarch	50 g / 2 oz
2½ cups	Milk	600 ml / 1 pint
	Salt and pepper	

1. Heat the butter in a small pan over a low heat, do not allow to brown. As soon as the butter has melted, stir in the flour and blend it vigorously with the butter to form a smooth mixture known as a roux, which should take on a pinkish colour.
2. Immediately add the milk, whisking or stirring briskly with a wooden spoon. Season with salt and white pepper to taste and cook until you have a thick pouring consistency. Do not leave a white sauce on the stove unattended. It will burn on the bottom of the pan and spoil the sauce.

Cook's tip: it is essential to season this sauce well or the vegetable, fish or poultry served with it will be bland.
For a thick sauce add a further 2 tablespoons [15 g / ½ oz] butter and flour to the recipe.

Ragu alla cacciatora

Beef Sauce for Pasta and Gnocchi

	00:10		01:40	

American	Ingredients	Metric/Imperial
1	Onion	1
1	Carrot	1
1	Celery stalk	1
¼ cup	Butter	50 g / 2 oz
⅓ cup	Oil	5 tbsp
1 oz	Dried mushrooms	25 g / 1 oz
1	Garlic clove	1
1 cup	Ground (minced) beef	225 g / 8 oz
	Salt and pepper	
½ cup	Red wine	125 ml / 4 fl oz
1 lb	Peeled tomatoes	450 g / 1 lb
1	Bay leaf	1

1. Finely chop onion, carrot and celery. Melt butter and oil and sauté vegetables for 2 minutes. Soak mushrooms in hot water and when soft, chop coarsely and add to the pan with a peeled crushed clove of garlic.

2. Cook these ingredients together for about 5 minutes then add the meat, salt and pepper and brown thoroughly.

3. Pour in the wine, then add the tomatoes. Crush a bay leaf and add to the sauce. Cover and simmer over a low heat for about 1½ hours.

Cook's tip: this sauce can be frozen for up to 6 months.

To freeze: cool, quickly pour into small containers, cover, seal and label.

To reheat: from frozen put in a moderate oven for 45 minutes or reheat in a saucepan over a very low heat.

In a microwave, select thaw or defrost setting and stir from time to time. Cook on 'High' for 3-4 minutes.

Salsa per pasta

Hot Sauce for Pasta

00:20 00:20

American	Ingredients	Metric/Imperial
1	Large onion	1
¼ cup	Butter	50 g / 2 oz
	Pinch of salt	
1 tsp	Flour	1 tsp
1 cup	Whipping (double) cream	225 ml / 8 fl oz
¼ cup	Brandy	50 ml / 2 fl oz
1	Red chilli pepper	1
2 lb	Ripe tomatoes	1 kg / 2 lb
1 lb	Shell pasta	450 g / 1 lb
½ cup	Grated parmesan cheese	50 g / 2 oz
	Few fresh basil leaves	

1. Finely chop the onion, heat butter and sauté the onion until soft but not brown. Sprinkle with salt, add the flour and cook for 2 minutes, stirring with a wooden spoon.

2. Allow to cool slightly then mix in the cream and bring to the boil, stirring with a wooden spoon until the sauce thickens, then add the brandy and deseeded chopped chilli.

3. Peel and sieve all but 6 of the tomatoes, adding the sieved mixture to the sauce.

4. Meanwhile, cook the pasta in boiling salted water. When the pasta is 'al dente', drain and pour into the pan containing the sauce, add parmesan, cut the remaining tomatoes into strips and add these with the chopped basil leaves to the sauce. Allow the pasta to absorb the sauce for a few minutes over a low heat, then serve.

Salsa besciamella 〰️

Béchamel Sauce

🔪 00:20   00:20 🍲

American	Ingredients	Metric/Imperial
2½ cups	Milk	600 ml / 1 pint
1	Medium-sized onion	1
1	Small carrot	1
1	Bay leaf	1
1	Bouquet garni	1
8	Peppercorns	8
3 tbsp	Butter	40 g / 1½ oz
6 tbsp	Flour	40 g / 1½ oz
	Salt and pepper	
3 tbsp	Coffee (single) cream (optional)	2 tbsp

1. Pour the milk into a saucepan, add the peeled and quartered onion, a scraped and roughly chopped carrot, bay leaf, bouquet garni and peppercorns. Heat gently over a very low heat. When the milk looks as if it is about to boil turn off the heat, cover and leave to infuse for 15 minutes.
2. Heat the butter in a saucepan over a low heat, do not allow to brown. Tip in the sieved flour and mix well to make a roux, cook for at least 1 minute then strain in the infused milk whisking or stirring briskly with a wooden spoon.
3. Continue cooking, stirring all the time to prevent lumps forming, until a thick pouring sauce is made. Taste and season, add cream for a rich sauce. Use for vegetables, fish, eggs and pasta dishes.

Besciamella allo scalogno 〰️〰️

Shallot Béchamel

🔪 00:10   00:10 🍲

American	Ingredients	Metric/Imperial
⅓ cup	Butter	75 g / 3 oz
¾ cup	Cornstarch (cornflour)	75 g / 3 oz
5 cups	Milk	1.2 litres / 2 pints
¼ lb	Shallots or small onion	100 g / 4 oz

1. Melt butter, add cornstarch, and cook for 2 minutes. Cool slightly, then pour in the milk and bring to the boil stirring all the time. Finely chop shallots and add to the sauce. Simmer for another 3-4 minutes.
2. Serve sauce with crunchy cooked vegetables or with left-over pasta and rice.

Variation
1. Substitute a finely chopped onion for the shallots.
2. 1 tablespoon vodka can be added to the sauce.

Cook's tip: cover sauce with film whilst cooling to prevent a skin forming.

Salsa con le noci

Walnut Béchamel Sauce

▭▭▶ 00:10   00:10 ◀▭

American	Ingredients	Metric/Imperial
1 cup	Shelled walnuts	100 g / 4 oz
1 cup	Béchamel sauce	225 ml / 8 fl oz
1	Egg yolk	1
3 tbsp	Grated parmesan cheese	2 tbsp

1. Shell the walnuts and blanch them for a few minutes to facilitate peeling. Remove as much of the membrane as possible and finely chop.
2. Pour the béchamel sauce into a saucepan and add the chopped walnuts and egg yolk.
3. Stir the béchamel sauce vigorously with a wooden spoon to obtain a smooth creamy sauce.
4. Place the saucepan over a low heat and then cook the sauce for 10 minutes stirring constantly, but do not allow to boil. Finally, mix in the grated parmesan.
5. Serve with spaghetti or to accompany pansotti.

Ragu

Bolognese Sauce

▭▭▶ 00:15   01:15 ◀▭

American	Ingredients	Metric/Imperial
1	Carrot	1
1	Medium-sized onion	1
1	Celery stalk	1
2½ oz	Bacon	65 g / 2½ oz
2 tbsp	Butter	25 g / 1 oz
Scant ¼ cup	Olive oil	3 tbsp
5 oz	Sausage meat	150 g / 5 oz
1 cup	Ground (minced) beef	225 g / 8 oz
½ cup	Red wine	125 ml / 4 fl oz
1 cup	Tomato sauce (see page 79)	225 ml / 8 fl oz
½ cup	Stock	125 ml / 4 fl oz
	Salt and pepper	

1. Finely chop the carrot, onion, celery and bacon. Heat the butter and oil in a saucepan over a low heat, and sauté prepared vegetables until golden brown.
2. Break the sausage meat up with a fork and add to the beef and stir thoroughly. After a few minutes, pour in red wine and allow to evaporate, keeping the heat turned low.
3. When all the wine has evaporated, pour in the tomato sauce and the hot stock. Stir in and leave to simmer for at least 1 hour over a low heat, stirring from time to time with a wooden spoon. If the sauce becomes too dry, add more stock.
4. Finally taste and adjust seasoning, adding salt if necessary and freshly milled pepper and cook for a further 5 minutes.
5. Serve with tagliatelle (made with eggs), spaghetti and other pasta. Coarsely chopped mushrooms may be added to the chopped vegetables if wished.

Salsa alle nocciole

Hazelnut Sauce

American	Ingredients	Metric/Imperial
1	Garlic clove	1
3 tbsp	Oil	2 tbsp
1	Anchovy	1
1 cup	Hazelnuts	100 g / 4 oz
3 tbsp	Grated parmesan cheese	2 tbsp
1 lb	Spaghetti	450 g / 1 lb

1. Crush garlic, heat oil and cook garlic over a low heat. Remove garlic from pan when it begins to brown.
2. Clean anchovy and chop into small pieces, add to the oil and cook for 1 minute stirring with a wooden spoon. Remove from heat.
3. Grate or blend hazelnuts with the parmesan, mixing well and put directly into a serving dish.
4. Cook spaghetti until 'al dente' (8-10 minutes), drain, and put in serving dish. Mix in the nuts and parmesan, then pour over the oil and serve hot.

Salsa con le noci

Walnut Sauce

American	Ingredients	Metric/Imperial
3½ cups	Shelled walnuts	400 g / 14 oz
1 cup	Stock	225 ml / 8 fl oz
	Salt	
1 cup	Coffee (single) cream	225 ml / 8 fl oz

1. Shell walnuts and keep kernels as whole as possible. Blanch in boiling water, then peel and remove membranes.
2. Place in a food processor, add half the stock and process to a creamy pulp. (A pestle and mortar can be used instead.)
3. Transfer to a saucepan and stir in the remaining stock. Season with salt and cook over a low heat, until the mixture has thickened, then strain. Collect purée in the saucepan, stir in cream and place over a low heat to warm the cream. Serve immediately with pasta.

Salsa col mascarpone

Mascarpone Sauce

| | 00:15 | 00:00 |

American	Ingredients	Metric/Imperial
3 oz	Mascarpone cheese	75 g / 3 oz
1	Egg yolk	1
2 oz	Raw ham	50 g / 2 oz
3 tbsp	Grated parmesan cheese	2 tbsp
	Salt and pepper	

1. Whisk together the mascarpone cheese and the egg yolk in a bowl. Cut the ham into thin strips and add this to the mixture together with the parmesan, salt and pepper.
2. Stir ingredients well together and add 1 tablespoon boiling water (for convenience use the water from the pasta). Then beat thoroughly with a wooden spoon until the mixture becomes soft and light.
3. Serve with pasta such as fettucine.

Salsa al pomodoro

Tomato Sauce

| | 00:30 | 00:50 |

American	Ingredients	Metric/Imperial
2 lb	Tomatoes	1 kg / 2 lb
1 tbsp	Oil	1 tbsp
2 tbsp	Butter	25 g / 1 oz
1	Onion	1
2	Garlic cloves	2
1	Carrot	1
1 tbsp	Flour	1 tbsp
2 lb	Tomatoes	1 kg / 2 lb
½ tsp	Basil	½ tsp
1	Bay leaf	1
½ tsp	Thyme	½ tsp
½ tsp	Sugar	½ tsp
	Salt and pepper	
1 tbsp	Tomato purée	1 tbsp
½ cup	White wine (optional)	125 ml / 4 fl oz

1. Plunge the tomatoes into boiling water, remove the skins and drain.
2. Heat the oil and butter in a pan over a low heat, add the peeled and finely chopped onion and the crushed garlic. Allow to cook for 5 minutes, stirring from time to time. Add the grated carrot, stir for 1 minute then add the flour and stir well until the vegetables have absorbed it.
3. Add the remaining ingredients with 1 cup [225 ml / 8 fl oz] water and the wine, allow to simmer for 45 minutes on a low heat. Remove bay leaf and sprigs of herbs before serving or using in other dishes.

Cook's tip: for a smooth tomato sauce, pass through a sieve, blender or food processor.

Salsa ai granchi

Crab Sauce

⊏▭⊐ 00:15   00:35 to 00:40
                   using fresh crab
                   00:20 using canned crab

American	Ingredients	Metric/Imperial
3 oz	Crab	75 g / 3 oz
1	Garlic clove	1
2 tbsp	Butter	25 g / 1 oz
1 tbsp	Olive oil	1 tbsp
1 tsp	Anchovy paste	1 tsp
1 cup	Tomato sauce (see page 79)	225 ml / 8 fl oz
1	Bunch of parsley	1

1. If using canned crab, drain off liquid. If fresh, boil crab allowing 15 minutes per 1 lb / 450 g, then finely dice and set aside.
2. Crush the garlic. Heat butter and oil in a pan over a low heat, and add garlic. When it begins to brown, remove from the pan and add anchovy paste, dissolved in the tomato sauce.
3. Simmer for 15 minutes, add crab and chopped parsley, then remove from the heat after a few minutes.
4. Serve with spaghetti or tagliatelle.

Salsa al gorgonzola

Gorgonzola Sauce

⊏▭⊐ 00:10   00:10

American	Ingredients	Metric/Imperial
2 oz	Mild gorgonzola cheese	50 g / 2 oz
3 oz	Mature gorgonzola cheese	75 g / 3 oz
⅔ cup	Butter	125 g / 5 oz
5 tbsp	Coffee (single) cream	4 tbsp
3 tbsp	Brandy	2 tbsp

1. Finely dice both gorgonzolas, put into a bowl and crush with a fork to blend together. Add half the butter and continue beating with a wooden spoon to obtain a smooth paste.
2. Melt remaining butter in a saucepan and add gorgonzola mixture. Mix and warm over a low heat for a few minutes. Remove from the heat, add cream and brandy.
3. Serve with plain risotto by pouring over and mixing in well just before serving. This sauce can also be served with gnocchi.

Salsa di pomodoro con fegatini

Tomato and Chicken Liver Sauce

| | 00:20 | 00:35 |

American	Ingredients	Metric/Imperial
½	Onion	½
2 oz	Raw ham	50 g / 2 oz
2 tbsp	Butter	25 g / 1 oz
1 cup	Fresh mushrooms	100 g / 4 oz
2 oz	Chicken livers	50 g / 2 oz
1 cup	Tomato sauce (see page 79)	225 ml / 8 fl oz
	Salt and pepper	
1	Small bunch of parsley	1
½ cup	Dry red wine	125 ml / 4 fl oz

1. Finely chop the onion and cut the ham into thin strips. Heat these in the butter in a saucepan and cook over a very low heat for about 10 minutes.
2. Thickly slice the mushrooms, add to the pan and cook for a few minutes stirring with a wooden spoon.
3. Coarsely chop the chicken livers and add to the other ingredients together with the tomato sauce and a little pepper. Stir and bring to the boil. Boil for a few seconds then turn down the heat again and simmer for 15 minutes, stirring constantly.
4. Chop the parsley. Heat the wine in another saucepan and reduce by a half. Add this to the sauce with the parsley.
5. Serve with cooked tagliatelle or any other pasta.

Pesto alla genovese

Garlic and Basil Sauce

| | 00:30 | 00:00 |

American	Ingredients	Metric/Imperial
¼ lb	Fresh basil	100 g / 4 oz
1 oz	Marjoram	25 g / 1 oz
1 oz	Parsley	25 g / 1 oz
1	Garlic clove	1
¼ cup	Mixed grated pecorino and parmesan cheeses	25 g / 1 oz
6 tbsp	Olive oil	5 tbsp

1. Crush basil, marjoram, parsley and garlic using a pestle and mortar, blender or food processor. Add pecorino and parmesan. Continue to crush and add oil in a thin trickle. Taste and adjust seasoning. Serve with pasta.

Variation: the marjoram can be omitted, and parsley reduced to half the quantity.

Salsa diablotin

Devilled Sauce

🔪 00:10　　　　　00:10 🥘

American	Ingredients	Metric/Imperial
2	Shallots	2
½ cup	Full-bodied red wine	125 ml / 4 fl oz
3 tbsp	Vinegar	2 tbsp
Scant ¼ cup	Flour	25 g / 1 oz
2	Egg yolks	2
	Red chilli powder	
¼ cup	Brandy	50 ml / 2 fl oz

1. Finely chop the shallots and put in a saucepan with the wine and the vinegar over a high heat and boil uncovered until half the liquid has evaporated.
2. Liquidize in a blender and stir in the flour before pouring back into the saucepan. Bring to the boil, stirring continuously to obtain a smooth sauce.
3. Remove the sauce from the heat and continue stirring with a wooden spoon.
4. Beat in the egg yolks, pinch of chilli powder and the brandy until well mixed.
5. Pour the warm sauce into a sauceboat and serve.

Salsa di mare

Seafood Sauce

🔪 00:20   01:05 🥘

American	Ingredients	Metric/Imperial
½ lb	Scorpion fish	225 g / 8 oz
¼ lb	Prawns	100 g / 4 oz
5 oz	Squid	150 g / 5 oz
5	Peppercorns	5
1	Garlic clove	1
1	Small bunch of parsley	1
Scant ¼ cup	Olive oil	3 tbsp
1 cup	Tomato sauce (see page 79)	225 ml / 8 fl oz
	Red chilli pepper powder	
	Salt and pepper	

1. Carefully wash and clean all the fish, leaving the head on the scorpion fish, and the prawns unpeeled. Cut the squid into pieces. Fill a saucepan with 1 quart [1 litre / 1¾ pints] water add the peppercorns and bring to the boil First put in the squid and then after 10 minutes, add the scorpion fish and prawns. Boil for another 10 minutes.
2. When the fish is cooked, remove from the water. Strain the fish stock and reserve for the risotto. Peel the prawns and remove the head, the tail and the backbone from the scorpion fish. Then finely chop the prawns, scorpion fish and squid together. Put in a bowl and crush with a fork to form a smooth paste.
3. Finely chop the garlic and parsley and heat in the oil in a saucepan. Add fish mixture, tomato sauce, and pinch of chilli powder. Simmer over a low heat for about 30 minutes, stirring from time to time with a wooden spoon. Taste and adjust seasoning.
4. While the sauce is simmering, prepare a white risotto in a separate saucepan using the fish stock. When the rice is cooked, pour over the fish sauce, mix and serve immediately. The sauce can also be served with pasta.

Sughi per bollito misto

Green and Red Sauces for Mixed Meat Dishes

00:35
Standing time 02:00 to 03:00

00:00

American	Ingredients	Metric/Imperial
Green sauce		
1	Large bunch of parsley	1
1	Hard-cooked (boiled) egg	1
	The inside of a bread roll	
3 tbsp	Vinegar	2 tbsp
½	Sweet red pepper	½
½	Sweet yellow pepper	½
4	Anchovies in salt	4
	Salt	
½ cup	Virgin olive oil	125 ml / 4 fl oz
1	Garlic clove	1
Red sauce		
1 lb	Tomatoes	500 g / 1 lb
1	Onion	1
1	Sweet green pepper	1
1	Carrot	1
1	Celery stalk	1
1 tbsp	Basil	1 tbsp
	Salt	
1	Chilli pepper	1
1 tsp	Olive oil	1 tsp

Green Sauce

1. Clean the parsley, remove the stalks, rinse thoroughly and dry. Shell the egg, soak the bread in the vinegar and when the vinegar has been absorbed, squeeze it out by hand. Wash the sweet pepper, remove the seeds and filaments, and then cut them lengthways into thin strips. Wash and fillet the anchovies. Place all the ingredients together on a large chopping board, and chop them very finely.

2. Transfer the chopped ingredients to a bowl, add salt to taste, and stir in the olive oil to obtain the right consistency. Halve the garlic clove and add it to the sauce. Leave for a few hours for the flavours to infuse, and then remove the garlic. If the garlic is to be retained in the sauce, chop it finely with the other ingredients before adding the olive oil.

Red Sauce

1. Clean, wash and coarsely chop the tomatoes, onion, sweet pepper, carrot, celery and basil.

2. Heat all these ingredients together in a covered pan over a low heat, adding a little water if there is not enough liquid from the tomatoes.

3. When cooked, rub through a sieve, return to pan and continue cooking, stirring frequently. Season with salt. Just before serving, remove from heat, crumble in the chilli and stir in a trickle of oil.

4. Serve thickened sauce either hot or cold.

Cook's tip: if you wish, the ingredients for the green sauce can be finely chopped in a blender or food processor before adding the olive oil.

Salsa alle vongole
Clam Sauce

American	Ingredients	Metric/Imperial
20	Clams	20
1 cup	White wine	225 ml / 8 fl oz
½	Onion	½
1	Celery stalk	1
2 tbsp	Butter	25 g / 1 oz
¼ cup	Flour	25 g / 1 oz
¼ cup	Brandy	50 ml / 2 fl oz

1. Clean the clams thoroughly then put in a pan with the white wine. Cover and boil for a few minutes until the clams have opened.

2. Remove pan from the heat and remove the clams from their shells. Leave to cool and then chop finely and reserve. Strain the stock and keep it warm over a low heat.

3. Finely chop the onion and celery and sauté in butter in a saucepan, until onion is golden.

4. Stir in the flour mixing vigorously to obtain a roux. Cool slightly then gradually pour in the hot stock, stirring vigorously to stop the sauce becoming lumpy. Cook for at least 3-4 minutes until the sauce is thick and creamy. Mix in the chopped clams and the brandy. Stir and continue cooking over a low heat for another 5 minutes.

5. Serve the sauce with pasta.

Al tonno e ai piselli
Tuna and Pea Sauce

American	Ingredients	Metric/Imperial
1	Medium-sized onion	1
Scant ¼ cup	Olive oil	3 tbsp
1 cup	Tomato juice	225 ml / 8 fl oz
14 oz	Fresh peas, unshelled	400 g / 14 oz
¼ lb	Tuna	100 g / 4 oz
1 cup	Stock	225 ml / 8 fl oz
	Salt and pepper	

1. Peel and finely chop the onion. Heat oil and sauté onion until it begins to turn golden. Add the tomato juice and simmer for a few minutes.

2. Shell the peas, add to the pan and continue to simmer for 15 minutes, adding a little stock if tomato juice has reduced too much. Stir from time to time.

3. When the peas are cooked, break up drained tuna fish with a fork and add to the pan. Cook for 5 minutes then taste and adjust seasoning.

4. Serve with pasta.

Salsa ai gamberetti

Shrimp Sauce

	00:15	00:20

American	Ingredients	Metric/Imperial
¾ lb	Shrimps	350 g / 12 oz
5 tbsp	Butter	65 g / 2½ oz
3 tbsp	Flour	2 tbsp
Scant ¼ cup	Tomato sauce	3 tbsp
¼ cup	White wine	50 ml / 2 fl oz
	Salt and pepper	

1. Wash but do not peel the shrimps. Put them into a saucepan, cover with cold water and bring to the boil. Simmer for 5 minutes to obtain a little fish stock to use later. Drain and peel the shrimps taking care not to break them, and reserve.
2. Heat half the butter in a saucepan and, when it has melted, stir in the flour. Cook over a moderate heat for 2 minutes. Cool slightly then gradually pour in the hot fish stock and continue stirring while adding the tomato sauce. Bring to the boil, then continue cooking over a very low heat for about 3 minutes, stirring continuously. Finally, taste and adjust seasoning and remove from the heat.
3. In another saucepan, melt the remaining butter and add the shrimps. Sauté over a low heat and pour in the wine. Allow the wine to evaporate over a moderate heat then pour the tomato sauce over the shrimps, add a little freshly milled pepper and continue cooking for another 10 minutes stirring frequently with a wooden spoon. Serve with pasta.

Salsa di cozze

Mussel Sauce

	00:20	00:20

American	Ingredients	Metric/Imperial
10	Mussels	10
1	Medium-sized onion	1
1	Small bunch of parsley	1
2 tbsp	Butter	25 g / 1 oz
¼ cup	Flour	25 g / 1 oz
	Salt and pepper	

1. Clean the mussels thoroughly and finely chop the onion. Put these in a frying pan together with a few sprigs of parsley. Cover with water and heat. After about 5 minutes, the mussels should have opened indicating that they are cooked. Strain the stock, and make up 2 cups [225 ml / 8 fl oz] with water.
2. Remove the mussel shells and finely chop the mussels into an earthenware bowl.
3. Melt the butter in a saucepan and as soon as it begins to sizzle, stir in the flour. Mix vigorously with a wooden spoon, allow to cool then gradually stir in the hot stock using a ladle to measure it out. Stir constantly to prevent lumps forming and bring to the boil. Reduce heat and simmer for 2-3 minutes. Taste and adjust seasoning, add a little chopped parsley and the chopped mussels. Cook for another 5 minutes. Finally, taste and adjust the seasoning, and serve with pasta.

SOUPS

SOUPS

Minestra di zucchine

Courgette Soup

🔪	00:15	00:35 🍳

American	Ingredients	Metric/Imperial
3 tbsp	Vegetable oil	2 tbsp
1	Sliced onion	1
6	Zucchini (courgettes)	6
2	Potatoes	2
12	Peeled tomatoes	12
2 quarts	Stock	2 litres / 3½ pints
¾ lb	Pasta	350 g / 12 oz
¼ tsp	Nutmeg	¼ tsp
3	Sprigs of parsley	3

1. Heat the oil in a large saucepan, add the chopped onion and cook for 3 minutes.
2. Wash and dice the zucchini, peel and dice the potatoes.
3. Add the tomatoes to the onion and then stir in the zucchini and the potatoes, allow to brown over a medium heat for a few minutes.
4. Add the stock and cook for 10 minutes, throw in the pasta and cook until it is 'al dente'.
5. Sprinkle with grated nutmeg and chopped parsley, serve.

Minestra campagnola

Country Soup

🔪	00:15	00:45 🍳

American	Ingredients	Metric/Imperial
3	Plum tomatoes, fresh or canned	3
1	Onion	1
Scant ¼ cup	Vegetable oil	3 tbsp
	Salt and pepper	
2½ cups	Stock	600 ml / 1 pint
14 oz	Fresh pasta	400 g / 14 oz
2	Eggs	2
½ cup	Grated parmesan cheese	50 g / 2 oz
1 tbsp	Chopped parsley	1 tbsp

1. Scald the tomatoes in boiling water, drain them, peel and cut into strips, removing the seeds. Peel and finely chop the onion.
2. Heat the oil in a large pan, sweat the onion until transparent over a low heat, add tomatoes, seasoning, 1 cup [225 ml / 8 fl oz] water and continue cooking gently for 20 minutes.
3. Add the stock to the pan, bring to the boil and throw in the pasta. Cook for 8 minutes, lower heat.
4. Whisk the eggs, flavor with a pinch of seasoning, the parmesan and the chopped parsley. Add some hot soup to the egg then mix together and pour into the pan with the pasta a few moments before removing from the heat. Stir, allow the eggs to thicken the soup, then transfer to a heated tureen.

Minestrone alla genovese

Genoese Minestrone

	01:00	01:00
	Soaking time for dried beans 12:00	

American	Ingredients	Metric/Imperial
¼ lb	Dried beans	100 g / 4 oz
4 tbsp	Olive oil	3 tbsp
1	Onion	1
1	Celery stalk	1
1	Slice of raw ham	1
1	Small savoy cabbage	1
2	Carrots	2
6	Swiss chard leaves	6
6	Lettuce leaves	6
1 tbsp	Tomatoe purée	1 tbsp
2 quarts	Stock	2 litres / 1¾ pints
2	Garlic cloves	2
5	Sprigs of parsley	5
3	Basil leaves	3
3	Rosemary leaves	3
½ cup	Grated parmesan cheese	50 g / 2 oz
1	Chilli pepper	1
½ lb	Pasta	225 g / 8 oz

1. Boil the beans in lightly salted water; if using dried beans, leave them soaking in warm water for 12 hours.

2. Pour half the oil into a soup pan over a low heat and put in the chopped onion, celery and the ham cut into thin strips and allow to cook until golden.

3. Add cabbage, chopped carrots, chard and the washed lettuce cut into thin strips, the boiled beans and finally 1 tablespoon of tomato purée. Pour the stock into the pan, bring to the boil and simmer.

4. Meanwhile chop some garlic with the parsley and a few leaves of basil and rosemary, then add grated parmesan, chilli pepper and remaining oil. Reduce these ingredients to a pulp by crushing vigorously and then sieve them. (This can be done in a blender or food processor.)

5. As soon as the vegetables are ready, add the pasta, also mixing in the 'pulp'. Stir, and when the pasta is still rather firm, sprinkle with parmesan. Serve after a few minutes.

Minestrone al pesto

Minestrone with Garlic and Basil Sauce

	00:40	
	Soaking time 12:00	00:60

American	Ingredients	Metric/Imperial
5 oz	Haricot beans	150 g / 5 oz
1 oz	Dried mushrooms	25 g / 1 oz
2	Eggplant (aubergines)	2
¼ lb	Green beans	100 g / 4 oz
3	Potatoes	3
1	Red cabbage	1
¼ lb	Zucchini (courgettes)	100 g / 4 oz
2 oz	Pumpkin	50 g / 2 oz
4	Peeled tomatoes	4
3 tbsp	Vegetable oil	2 tbsp
2 oz	Pasta or rice	50 g / 2 oz
	Garlic and basil sauce	

1. Allow beans to soak overnight and soak dried mushrooms.
2. Bring 2 quarts [2 litres / 3½ pints] water to the boil and put in the beans and cook for 40 minutes. Dice the eggplant and green beans. Peel and dice the potatoes, and slice and chop the red cabbage. Slice the zucchini and dice the pumpkin. Add the vegetables, the peeled tomatoes, oil and dried mushrooms to the beans. Season well. When the ingredients are almost cooked, put in the pasta or rice, according to choice.
3. Before serving the soup, add a good helping of the garlic and basil sauce to the pan. Serve very hot.

Cook's tip: this also makes an excellent cold dish, which will keep for several days.

Minestra di fagioli alla bolognese

Bolognaise Bean Soup

	02:00	
	Soaking time 12:00	01:30

American	Ingredients	Metric/Imperial
7 oz	Dried beans	200 g / 7 oz
	Salt and pepper	
2 or 3	Garlic cloves	2 or 3
3 tbsp	Olive oil	2 tbsp
1	Small bunch of parsley	1
¾ lb	Very ripe tomatoes, puréed or	350 g / 12 oz
1¼ cups	Tomato sauce (see page 79)	300 ml / ½ pint
¾ lb	Pasta	350 g / 12 oz
½ cup	Grated grana cheese	50 g / 2 oz

1. Soak the dried beans overnight in cold water. The following day put them in 2 quarts [2 litres / 3½ pints] of cold water and boil, adding salt at the end of cooking. When beans are quite tender, drain and reserve the water.

2. Fry garlic in a pan with heated olive oil. As soon as the garlic is browned, add a little chopped parsley, the tomato purée and the boiled beans. Cook for 15 minutes, then add the cooking water from the beans.

3. At this point you can proceed in different ways, either sieve or blend (liquidize) everything, or leave the beans whole. Alternatively, sieve only half of them; this is a matter of personal taste.

4. When the soup begins to boil, throw in the pasta. Allow to cook, pour into a soup tureen and accompany it with a generous portion of grated cheese, chopped parsley and pepper to taste.

Minestrone toscano

Tuscan Minestrone

	00:30	01:40
American	**Ingredients**	**Metric/Imperial**
11 oz	Shelled white beans	300 g / 11 oz
2 oz	Parsley	50 g / 2 oz
1	Small onion	1
1	Celery stalk	1
2	Small carrots	2
1	Sprig of rosemary	1
2	Basil leaves	2
1	Garlic clove	1
2 oz	Bacon	50 g / 2 oz
½ cup	Olive oil	125 ml / 4 fl oz
4	Tomatoes	4
½	Savoy cabbage	½
2 or 3	Thyme leaves	2 or 3
	Salt and pepper	
5 oz	Pasta	150 g / 5 oz

1. Boil the beans in plenty of water and add salt towards the end of the cooking time. When they are cooked, drain, reserving the cooking water, and sieve or blend half of them.

2. While the beans are cooking, prepare the other ingredients. Chop the parsley, onion, celery, peeled carrots, sprig of rosemary and the basil together with the garlic clove and the bacon.

3. Heat the oil in a large pan, add the vegetable and herb mixture, cook gently over a low heat for 5 minutes, then add the peeled and chopped tomatoes, shredded cabbage, thyme, the sieved and whole beans.

4. Add 2 quarts [2 litres / 3¼ pints] cooking water from the beans made up with water or stock. Season lightly with salt and pepper. Cook on a slow heat for 40 minutes, then add the cabbage and the pasta. Serve without cheese when the pasta is cooked.

Cook's tip: if using dried haricot beans, soak overnight before cooking.

Zuppa alla toscana

Tuscany Soup

	00:25		02:30
	Soaking time 12:00		

American	Ingredients	Metric/Imperial
¼ lb	Lentils	100 g / 4 oz
¼ lb	Dried beans	100 g / 4 oz
1	Garlic clove	1
1	Onion	1
3	Sage leaves	3
1	Sprig of rosemary	1
2 oz	Bacon	50 g / 2 oz
¼ cup	Butter	50 g / 2 oz
3 tbsp	Vegetable oil	2 tbsp
2 quarts	Stock	2 litres / 3 ½ pints
	Pasta	

1. Put the lentils and beans in water and leave to soak overnight; throw away those which float to the surface.
2. Finely chop the garlic, peeled onion, sage leaves, rosemary and the bacon. Mix together.
3. Sweat all these ingredients in the butter and oil in a large pan on a very low heat; they should be softened, but not fried. Add the drained lentils and beans, allow the flavors to mingle and cover with the stock, cooking for 2 hours.
4. Put the mixture through a blender or food processor. Dilute with more stock, if necessary. Throw in the pasta and cook until 'al dente'. Add a tablespoon of cold oil as the finishing touch to this robust but truly delicious dish.

Minestra di pasta e carciofi

Pasta and Artichoke Soup

	01:00		00:25

American	Ingredients	Metric/Imperial
6	Jerusalem artichokes	6
½	Lemon	½
2 tbsp	Butter	25 g / 1 oz
1	Small onion	1
1	Slice of lean bacon	1
2	Peeled tomatoes	2
	Salt and pepper	
5 oz	Fresh pasta	150 g / 5 oz
1 tbsp	Chopped parsley	1 tbsp
½ cup	Grated parmesan cheese or pecorino	50 g / 2 oz

1. Peel the artichokes and cut in half vertically and then into slices about 1 in / 2½ cm, then throw them into water made acid with lemon juice.
2. In a saucepan heat the butter, fry the chopped onion and bacon in the butter over a gentle heat. When they are

transparent and only lightly colored, add the slices of artichoke, well drained. Fry on a moderate heat.

3. Add well crushed peeled tomatoes, allow the flavors to mingle for a couple of minutes and moisten with 1 quart [1 litre / 1¾ pints] of water, adding salt.

4. Bring to the boil, drop in the fresh pasta, and complete cooking over a fairly even heat, adding a little water if necessary. Remove from the heat, season, add chopped parsley. Serve parmesan separately.

Minestra di broccoli alla romana

Roman-Style Broccoli Soup

00:30   01:00

American	Ingredients	Metric/Imperial
14 oz	Broccoli	400 g / 14 oz
2 oz	Bacon	50 g / 2 oz
1	Garlic clove	1
1 tsp	Lard	1 tsp
1 tbsp	Tomato purée	1 tbsp
2 cups	Stock	450 ml / 16 fl oz
	Salt and pepper	
¼ lb	Pork rind	100 g / 4 oz
7 oz	Spaghetti	200 g / 7 oz
	Grated parmesan cheese	

1. Divide the broccoli into small pieces, wash well and drain.

2. Mince or finely chop the bacon with a clove of garlic. Heat the lard in a saucepan, add the bacon and garlic and brown for a few minutes. Add tomato purée, the broccoli pieces, 2 cups [450 ml / 16 fl oz] of stock or water, salt and pepper, and cook on a low heat.

3. Meanwhile scrape the pork rind thoroughly, cover with water and heat in a saucepan, boil for 1 minute, drain and cut the rind into thin strips. Return to the heat, add 1 cup [225 ml / 8 fl oz] of water and boil until soft.

4. When the pieces of broccoli are still firm, add the rind together with its cooking juices and continue cooking for another 10 minutes. Taste and add salt and pepper if necessary. When the soup comes to the boil, add the spaghetti broken into small pieces. Serve with parmesan.

INDEX

B
Bambi-Style Pie   43
Bigoli with Sardines   30
Bucatini
   bucatini with teal   49
   dashing bucatini   42
Gaeta-style bucatini   38

C
Cannelloni
   granny's cannelloni   70
   Sicilian-style
      cannelloni   70
Cheese   12-15
   gorgonzola sauce   80
   green ravioli with
      ricotta   62
   macaroni au gratin   32
   mascarpone noodles   56
   mascarpone sauce   79
   parmesan ravioli   57
   pasta, with   18
   pasta with ricotta   43
   pasta with two
      cheeses   26
   Valtellina noodles   52
Coastal-Style Corzetti   29

F
Fusilli
   high summer fusilli   37
   Neapolitan-style fusilli   36

G
Gaeta-Style Bucatini   38
Gnocchi
   fried gnocchi without
      filling   63
   green gnocchi   68
   little semolina gnocchi
      with gourds   67
   Magdalene's little
      gnocchi   64
   potato gnocchi with
      cheese   65
   stringy gnocchi   67
   Veronese-style
      gnocchi   63
   yellow gnocchi   64
Gourds
   little semolina gnocchi
      with gourds   67
   penne with raw
      gourds   42
   rigatoni with gourds   50

H
Hare, Noodles with   25

L
Lasagne
   Ligurian-style green
      lasagne   69
   small lasagne and
      snails   72
   spicy lasagne   71
   springtime lasagne   72

M
Macaroni
   chiken livers and macaroni
      pie   45
   guitar macaroni   30
   macaroni au gratin   32
   macaroni with
      octopus   39
   macaroni with vodka   29
   Sicilian baked
      macaroni   27
   small macaroni mold   48
   springtime macaroni   28

N
Noodles
   golden noodles   56
   gratinated green
      noodles   54
   huntsman's noodles   24
   leghorn-style noodles   55
   mascarpone noodles   56
   noodles and fish   51
   noodles with caviar and
      cream   53
   noodles with hare   25
   noodles with mussels   52
   noodles with onion and
      leek   50
   roebuck noodles   54
   Russian-style noodles   51
   Valtellina noodles   52
   Venetian-style
      noodles   53

O
Octopus, Macaroni with   39

P
Pasta
   cheese with   18
   cooking   17
   making fresh pasta
      20-21
   onion pasta   27
   pasta and artichoke
      soup   92
   pasta and peas   31
   pasta shells with brussels
      sprouts   35
   pasta with cream and
      mushrooms   23
   pasta with ricotta   43
   pasta with sardines   40